Mindfulness Training

An Easy Guide to Quickly Relieve Stress, Anxiety and Feel Present in Everyday Situations

(Learning Buddhist Teachings on Awakening)

Samuel Baer

Published by Rob Miles

© **Samuel Baer**

All Rights Reserved

Mindfulness Training: An Easy Guide to Quickly Relieve Stress, Anxiety and Feel Present in Everyday Situations (Learning Buddhist Teachings on Awakening)

ISBN 978-1-990084-00-3

All rights reserved. No part of this guide may be reproduced in any form without permission in writing from the publisher except in the case of brief quotations embodied in critical articles or reviews.

Legal & Disclaimer

The information contained in this book is not designed to replace or take the place of any form of medicine or professional medical advice. The information in this book has been provided for educational and entertainment purposes only.

The information contained in this book has been compiled from sources deemed reliable, and it is accurate to the best of the Author's knowledge; however, the Author cannot guarantee its accuracy and validity and cannot be held liable for any errors or omissions. Changes are periodically made to this book. You must consult your doctor or get professional medical advice before using any of the suggested remedies, techniques, or information in this book.

Upon using the information contained in this book, you agree to hold harmless the Author from and against any damages, costs, and expenses, including any legal fees potentially resulting from the application of any of the information provided by this guide. This disclaimer applies to any damages or injury caused by the use and application, whether directly or indirectly, of any advice or information presented, whether for breach of contract, tort, negligence, personal injury, criminal intent, or under any other cause of action.

You agree to accept all risks of using the information presented inside this book. You need to consult a professional medical practitioner in order to ensure you are both able and healthy enough to participate in this program.

Table of Contents

INTRODUCTION 1

CHAPTER 1: MINDFULNESS 101 3

CHAPTER 2: THE MEDITATION PROCESS 8

CHAPTER 3: MINDFULNESS MEDITATION 20

CHAPTER 4: HOW MINDFULNESS PROVIDES ANXIETY AND STRESS RELIEF 25

CHAPTER 5: THE PRACTICAL GUIDE TO MINDFULNESS MEDITATIONS 32

CHAPTER 6: MORE MINDFUL MEDITATION TECHNIQUES 43

CHAPTER 7: LEARNING ABOUT JUDGEMENT 49

CHAPTER 8: CONTROL FEAR 55

CHAPTER 9: MINDLESSNESS VERSUS MINDFULNESS 62

CHAPTER 10: MINDFULNESS MEDITATION 71

CHAPTER 11: ELEVEN BUDDHIST TECHNIQUES FOR MINDFULNESS 81

CHAPTER 12: WHY DO YOU NEED IT IN YOUR LIFE? 90

CHAPTER 13: THE POWER OF YOGA 95

CHAPTER 14: WHY PRACTICE MINDFULNESS? 100

CHAPTER 15: LEARNING TO BE LESS JUDGMENTAL 105

CHAPTER 16: WHERE TO MEDITATING AT HOME 111

CHAPTER 17: QUICK AND SIMPLE TECHNIQUES FOR A BEGINNER'S PRACTICE 116

CHAPTER 18: MEDITATION CAN HELP YOU ACHIEVE YOUR GOAL 129

CHAPTER 19: MINDFULNESS TECHNIQUES 133

CHAPTER 20: PRACTISING MINDFULNESS MEDITATION 150

CHAPTER 21: WHAT IS MINDFULNESS? 153

CHAPTER 22: BREATHING TECHNIQUES 158

CHAPTER 23: HOW TO PRACTICE MINDFUL MEDITATION 173

CHAPTER 24: SIMPLE EXERCISE TO START WITH 178

CHAPTER 25: MINDFULNESS MEDITATION STEP-BY-STEP 183

CONCLUSION 189

Introduction

This book contains proven steps and strategies on how to attain a deep state of mindfulness--a state where you can free yourself from mental clutter and embrace life's harmony and tranquility.

Begin your journey by knowing what mindfulness and meditation really are and how they can benefit you. Then, get to know what preparations you need to make for this practice—from finding the right time and setting up the right environment, to assuming the correct body posture and cultivating the right attitudes to help you tap into your inner being.

You can discover how you can easily attain the full benefits of this practice through different mindfulness exercises designed for beginners like you. Learn how to clear your mind, improve your concentration, relax your body and attain an overall feeling of peace and calmness. Also in this book are several techniques on how to deal with distractions so you can sustain a deep state of mindfulness all the way through your sessions.

Thanks again for downloading this book, I hope you enjoy it!

Chapter 1: Mindfulness 101

Be honest – how frequently do you pay attention and how much of it do you give to the things you do on a daily or moment-by-moment basis? I bet you'll answer "very little". I'll be surprised if you answered "I pay great attention to all if not most of the things I do everyday and every moment." You see, most of our actions and reactions need to be automatic or on autopilot if we want to keep up with today's fast-moving society. If we actually have to pay attention and think about each and every little thing we do, we won't get much done and get left behind.

Doing things on autopilot isn't necessarily bad. Like I wrote earlier, many of the things we need to do everyday have to be done unconsciously or automatically. Can you imagine yourself at 30 years old still having to think about how to tie your shoelaces or how to stand up and walk? Another important example of how important it is to do certain things automatically is writing or typing on the computer. It will be practically impossible to finish reports or write the things we need to write on a computer if we're not able to automatically type the letters and if we still do so by using one finger, one letter at the time.

But just because it's good doesn't mean it's absolutely good. Remember, even good things - if done excessively - can be harmful or bad. Too much food can make us obese. Too much rest makes us lethargic. Too much work can make us...well...dead! That being said, the best way to live is to achieve a great balance between living life on autopilot and being mindful of the things we do.

Simply put, mindfulness refers to a way of paying attention to what's happening in our lives and seeing them as they are without obstructions. For example, instead of simply getting the most conveniently available food, we can instead pay attention to the kinds of foods that are available and exercise our power to choose by going for healthier alternatives, though doing so may be more costly or inconvenient. Another good illustration of living mindfully is learning to say no to other people's requests or invitations instead of saying yes to them all the time. In particular, learning to say no to most invitations to party all night and paying attention to how we feel physically and even mentally the day after such parties.

To get a good grasp of what mindfulness living really is, keep these three things in mind.First, mindfulness requires being aware or paying more attention to some of the things we do or think. Second, mindfulness also involves acceptance of the things that we experience and by this I mean resisting the temptations to act automatically to either address or reject such things altogether. Oftentimes, doing so just makes things worse. And lastly, mindfulness living involves making wise choices. Part of choosing wisely includes the ability the separate our experiences from how we normally react to them. The more were able to do this, the wiser our choices become, particularly when it comes to things that can enhance our lives' joy, peace contentment.

Why Mindfulness?

Living mindfully can help us live lives that are much fuller and joyful. In particular, by helping us overcome depression, anxiety, and stress that our very busy lives and itineraries bring everyday. In particular, mindfulness living helps us do so by:

☐ Identifying and managing our habitual auto-reactions to much of our lives' events and circumstances more wisely;

☐ Helping us to more effectively manage and respond to complicated or challenging circumstances or situations in life;

☐ Enabling us to see our lives' circumstances more objectively and clearly;

☐ Allowing us to be more creative; and

☐ Helping us live more resilient and balanced lives.

While mindfulness can be a very effective tool to help us overcome depression, stress, and anxiety, it's not a tool for eliminating the things that cause such, a.k.a., "stressors".However, it helps us go a long way in terms of managing these things for optimal physical, emotional, and mental health.

Chapter 2: The Meditation Process

What can you expect to experience during the meditation process? You can expect to feel inner peace. You can expect to feel a certain sense of your energies flowing much more efficiently. Thus you feel a calm inside that helps you to really appreciate life and all that it has to offer. There was a famous author who went away to an Ashram to experience meditation. Elizabeth Gilbert found that she fought the idea of thinking of nothing at all and in the process found that the only way that she could gain from her meditative practice was to stop trying to fight it and let it happen. It took her a while, but when she did arrive at the point of seeing what the meditative process opened up to her, she was amazed at her own observation of life changing and her reach within herself becoming much more powerful than she ever thought possible.

The process involves being seated in a certain position, depending upon the type of meditation being practiced. It involves dropping the all invading thoughts that make your mind busy. For example, thoughts of the past serve no purpose. Some thoughts may be positive ones and these serve the purpose of nostalgia. However, in a meditative state, there is no past, there is no future – there is only now.

You may be asked to concentrate on your breathing techniques and be given different techniques to achieve different things. For example, if you are a stressed person, the breathing exercises that you experience during your meditation help you calm your mind and therefore concentrate on breathing deeply rather than hyper ventilating.

Those whose thoughts are depressive will be shown how to meditate and get rid of those depressing thoughts by replacing them, either with a mantra which is a repeated sequence of words or something to focus on to take all those negative thoughts away while feeling calm and away from distraction.

The meditative process may also involve looking inward and many people have trouble with this, just as Elizabeth Gilbert did. She found it boring at first and found that her thoughts flipped somersaults simply because someone had told her to think of nothing and she didn't see how she could. When you are able to meditate to this depth, the benefits are amazing. Don't expect it to happen straight away, but don't give up at first try either. She didn't and she reaped the benefits and you can too.

Pre-Meditation Practices That Help

These examples show you how you can break yourself into the meditation process. They are semi meditative in nature and will show you how your body can feel. In the first exercise, lie down on a comfortable bed and support your head with a comfortable pillow, so that your chin faces downward a little. This helps to open up the air passages so that your breathing is easier. You need to be away from noise. Quietude of mind takes quiet contemplation and this is where you begin to understand what meditation is all about. For this exercise, simply be aware of your breathing. Breathe in through the nose and count to six. Hold the breath inside you for the count of seven and then exhale being totally aware of the air leaving your body. This is a very good method because it teaches you self-control. It teaches you how to switch off and how to gain energy through meditative practice.

In another relaxation exercise that can prepare you for meditation, you can lie in a similar position and concentrate totally on each part of your body in turn, thinking of nothing else. Tense that part of the body and then feel it relax and go with the flow of the relaxation. From feet to the ankles, from the ankles to the knees and so forth until you have relaxed every part of your body.

The point of meditation is that it serves as a way to clear the mind of all things that use your brain's energies up. All of the negative thoughts that you have and all of the worries that this life gives you are all gone from your mind and in their place, you give your mind a peaceful haven where it can feel refreshed, energized and able to perform in a much better way. That's what the whole process of meditation is about and no matter which form you choose, you achieve the same aims because it makes you happier and more able to face the world in which you live with a positive attitude.

If you choose to take up yoga, you can combine contemplative yoga and meditation with more energetic Yoga poses that helps free up the flow of energy in your body, thus helping you to gain fitness for the body and for the mind. Think of meditation as yoga for the mind and you are pretty close to what happens when you practice it in a regular way and make it part and parcel of your life. You will be very glad you did and those few moments that it takes to meditate really help you to get through the rest of your day and night in a much more tranquil state of mind, thus stopping you from thinking negative things, and thus improving your lifestyle.

The Basic Practice

The basic idea of meditation is easy. All you need do is focus on the breath. This means that even as meditation takes on different forms, it all amounts to a central practice, the ability to focus on your breathing. Your mind might wander from time to time away from this, but all you need to do is directly bring your attention back to your breath. With the basic idea laid out, we can now explore the framework for your meditation practice.

Step One

•Follow the breath

As explained earlier, the first step towards meditation is to transport your attention to your breathing. Place your focus on the sensations surrounding it, the way air moves in and out of your system, the filling and draining of your stomach, the rise and fall of your chest.

Step Two

- Relax

Because we have the tendencies to store stress in ourselves, this step might be a bit challenging at first. But it is okay if you fail to attain full relaxation. With practice, it will get easier.

Each time you breathe out, let the tension flow out of your body. Focus on every breath and imagine this happening until you become entirely at ease and comfortable.

It may take some time at first, but with more practice, it will become easier to get rid of stress and delve into a relaxed state.

Step Three

- Focus your attention

For every kind of meditation, it is essential that you are focused, disciplined and can control your body. However, you cannot attain all of this within a single trial, but with practice, it will become faster.

Begin, by focusing on a single thing like your breath. However, it can be a candle, a mantra or some words of inspiration. Your mind will wander from time to time. Simply notice the triggers that distracted you, and then, slowly bring your attention back to your object of focus.

Step Four

- Expand your awareness

Meditation is all about attaining full consciousness. In reality, there are two essential elements of meditation and these two elements are connected. Whereas you can concentrate on a single object, you can also expand your mind, taking all things at once.

To expand your mind, simply let your awareness grow beyond your breath (or candle, etc.) and make it gradually spread to the rest of your body, and then to your mind, your emotions, your thoughts, and all other senses.

With each new area, watch as it absorbs your attention and then let it go and return to free and open awareness.

Step Five

- Exercise non-judgment

Sometimes, you may be tempted to judge yourself or others with each thought, memory, and feeling that flows through your awareness. Try not to judge them as anything – good, bad, right or wrong.

All you need do is to observe these actions without giving them any of such label. Do not try to control the kind of thoughts that flow through you at that moment, let your mind flow freely. Listen to it, the same way you would listen to the sound of the wind. Observe as your fantasies and memories begin to unfold. Remember, all of this does not define you, so sit back, relax and observe.

Step Six

- Share a connection with the Mind

The goal of meditation is not to silence or overcome the mind as it is popularly believed. What you are doing is simply training your mind to become a powerful tool in your defense.

Therefore, with each thought that seeks to distract you or capture your attention, do not try to resist, even unpleasant ones. Do not fight with your mind. Instead, watch this closely and notice the repetitive patterns of some thoughts. Such repeating thoughts or memories are only in place to teach you. Become friends with your mind and welcome each thought as they come, invited or not. The goal here is to understand your inner workings and establish the reasons for who or what you are.

Step Seven

- Let-go of your judgments

Your limiting beliefs, fears, worries, and judgments may fill your mind. All of these basic concepts you perceive as the things that shape your life may try to overturn you, giving you a picture that they are the ways you behave and connect to others.

They are not true. Simply smile and silently, refute them. They are only "stories," but they do not transform into who you are.

Step Eight

- Step away from your identity

A lot of us have this voice in our minds which are continually judging, analyzing, talking, planning, and remembering events and many more. They feel this is their mind, their ego, their personality.

With Meditation, you can let go of this lie and stop identifying with your ego. We can realize who we are and what we really are.

You are not your ego or your mind. You are vast, unlimited, and boundless. You are free and can do anything.

Step Nine

- Give in

This is the most delicate step, and yet, you will subtly enter this period. Also, it might be difficult during your first trial to achieve this essential step, but do not be alarmed, it will get comfortable with practice.

Meditation is about letting go of your fears, beliefs and those things you perceive as your gene make up. It is about surrendering every bit of it. It is crucial that you understand that you have to give up who you think you are to access who you can be. You have to give up what you think you know to permit the truth to abound.

So, when you sit down to practice, surrender how you feel, what you felt you should do and even your ideas about meditation. Make no expectations. Be open to whatever arises, give yourself to the stillness of the moment. Also, do not measure your progress against your set list of tasks or anyone else. Merely let the practice take you, surrender to it.

Chapter 3: Mindfulness Meditation

This action helps you a lot to develop your inner character and to see life from a more positive and realistic perspective. You will need to have twenty minutes a day to perform this, but it is life changing. You also need to ensure that you create a space where you can go to do your mindfulness meditation without interruption or without too much background noise, which will distract you. I tend to use first thing in the morning because it's a good time before the world has started to get up and make noise. If you need to set your alarm a little earlier to fit this into a busy life, then that's a good idea too. If you are alone in the winter of your life then choose a time spaced out from meals when you really can sit and pay attention, rather than using random times of day. The reason I say this is that you need to do this for 20 minutes every day and if you make it into a daily habit or routine, keeping the session at the same time, it's more likely to stick.

Sitting

Dressed in comfortable clothing that is not at all restrictive, sit on an upright chair, like a dining chair that is relatively hard and which encourages you to keep your back straight and your feet flat on the ground. Place your hands, one on top of the other on your lap and avoid playing with your fingers during the course of your session. Before you start meditation, let me explain what it's all about. It's allowing your mind to feel life through your senses. For example, you can feel how warm or cold a room is. You can hear with your ears, see with your eyes, touch with your hands and also use your mind. You also have the sense of taste. These are things we are too busy to notice much because life is too hectic, but during the course of your meditation, you may also find it a wonderful experience to have something scented near you so that you can soak in the aroma.

Breathing

Everyone knows how to breathe. Otherwise, they wouldn't be alive, but how often have you thought about proper breathing? Breathe in through your nostrils to the count of seven and then breathe out to the count of 10. The reason that you breathe out for longer than you breathe in is because you tend to over-oxygenate. People do that and it's not unusual, but you need to keep this level of breathing going until it becomes a good rhythm. During breathing in this manner, your body works better because you are using your full lung capacity instead of about a third of it – which is what people use with shallow breathing. It will bring down your heart rate and your blood pressure, so be aware when you finish your session that you need to relax for a moment and let these come back up again. Use this moment after meditating to write down how you feel and what you think you can do tomorrow that will improve the experience. Perhaps you heard noises and want to choose a quieter place. Perhaps you had a draft of wind come in from a window and want to move so that you are not distracted by it next time.

Meditation

Keep breathing in this way and try not to think of anything at all. Of course, the human mind will think of things and there's nothing that you can do to stop it. In fact, if you start to tell yourself off for thinking things, it goes against what meditation is all about. It's just about being mindful of what's going on and that means noticing it, dismissing it and then going back to concentrating on your breathing. Meditation helps you to let go of thoughts. You see them just like you would see a passing scene from a train. One moment it is there and then you let go because it's gone. The only time that you make those thoughts a problem is when you start to use emotions and other thoughts to string along from those original thoughts. Thus, if a thought comes, accept it and then let it go.

You may wonder what this does. A lot of people ask me and they keep asking even though they have had several sessions of meditation. What it does is quieten the mind and help it to find some kind of peace. When it happens, you will know that it has, but in the meantime be very happy that it gives you clarity of mind after the session is over. It also helps you to be able to deal with the thought processes that hinder your life and make you feel so bad. Meditation is like stopping the roundabout for a moment just so that you can breathe and not really think about anything in any great depth. Instead of having a mind full of confusion, you allow the mind to have peace. Being mindful away from meditation is slightly different, but I will explain this in a further chapter. Don't judge your progress. It isn't something to judge. In fact, if you do it daily for 20 minutes a day, you will find that the process of mindfulness will evolve for you in its own way. Just tell yourself to sit and breathe and concentrate on nothing except the breathing.

Chapter 4: How Mindfulness Provides Anxiety And Stress Relief

Mindfulness is a peaceful state of self-awareness when you are present in the moment and accept everything you experience within and around you for what it is without being even the least bit judgmental of it.

When you are completely mindful, your awareness lies only in the present moment and you become one with yourself and your surroundings and everything that happens to you or around you does not bother you. This state does sound wonderful, but how can it relieve stress and anxiety? Let us find that out.

The State of Life without Mindfulness

Most of us live on autopilot. Our mind usually seems to have an opinion and will of its own. Thoughts enter and leave our mind, and it seems as if we do not have much say on what thoughts we experience or the emotions we feel as a result of these thoughts. For instance, if you dislike something and feel angry as a result, you may think you don't have control over how you feel. If you could just stand back and observe your mind, you would find out how quickly your thoughts jump from one unfinished idea to another with the thoughts constantly interrupting one another and overlapping each other in a series of constant ideas, desires, memories and pictures.

As you skip from one thought to another, you often react to them based on your previous preconceived notions. Instead of deciphering each thought individually and free from any preconceived notion, you judge it based on your previous experiences and fail to analyze something for what it truly it is. This leads to undue stress, which only becomes worse with time if you do not do anything.

When you move from one thought to another and judge everything based on your preconceived notions, you fail to be present in the moment. In fact, you are doing the exact opposite of that and when you are not present peacefully and nonjudgmentally with the moment, the following starts to happen:

· You become stressed even when there is nothing to be stressed about. For instance, if your boss sternly speaks to you to be on time, you become stressed and start panicking that he may fire you the next time you are late because you start thinking of all the times he has previously warned you not to be late and think of the times when you delayed your work. If you just take it as a note of concern from your boss and stop thinking about the experiences associated with it, you will stop feeling extremely stressed and will focus more on what you can do in the moment - work hard and impress your boss with your good work.

- You start fearing things when there is nothing to be afraid of. If you are stuck in traffic, you are quite likely to think about being scolded by your boss for being late and when you keep thinking about this, your mind starts to become paralyzed with fear. If you nurture mindfulness, you will accept the traffic jam as a traffic jam and instead of thinking about what may happen, think of how you can best use that time at your disposal. You may start searching for an upcoming project on your phone or listen to music to unwind. This helps you relax instead of becoming stressed.

- You fail to enjoy the moment and be completely involved in the task. If you are playing with your child, you may keep thinking about the meal you have to prepare for the family or the fight you had with your spouse instead of enjoying time with your child. This keeps you from being happy in the moment and only increases your worry. When this happens when you are engaged in professional activities, you have more slip-ups than usual, which negatively affects your performance.

This state of not being mindful is known as forgetfulness and only increases your stress, tension and anxiety making you experience it for quite long.

Mindfulness Switches off Your Autopilot and Enables You to Experience Things as They Are

Things instantly change for the better when you nurture mindfulness. Mindfulness helps you remain in a constant state of attentiveness of the present moment that allows you to accept everything the way it happens and for what it is without associating any sort of label with it.

When you don't judge the different things happening to you or around you, you stop putting the 'good', 'bad', 'negative' and 'positive' labels on them and when you stop being them, you come into harmony with every existence and situation around you and every feeling inside you.

If your boss is angry because you were late, you accept it as his response to you being late for work and not as a personal remark. If you feel angry in response to his admonishing you, you accept that anger as a natural response to not receiving a nice comment and stop over-reacting to it. If you feel tensed for being stuck at something, you acknowledge that feeling and find out what you can do about it instead of just thinking about it repeatedly.

The moment you start accepting things for what they are, you stop blowing things out of proportion and since stress and anxiety are often the result of you making mountains out of molehills, both the responses dissipate away quicker than you think when you become mindful. Also, this realization helps you acknowledge stress and anxiety for what they are when you experience them without perceiving them as signs of your weakness.

Further, mindfulness allows you to live in the moment, enjoy it, relish it and make the best use of it. If you are cooking, cleaning, driving, playing, relaxing or doing anything else, you do it with full concentration and attentiveness instead of being elsewhere. This makes the task more enjoyable, which gives you a break from your mind being on autopilot. This is a great feeling to experience as it allows you to be one with the present moment and focus more on doing things now than living in the past or future.

Now that you have a clear understanding of how mindfulness rescues you from undue stress and anxiety, let me share with you some of the most effective mindfulness based techniques to calm down increased stress and anxiety.

Chapter 5: The Practical Guide To Mindfulness Meditations

How to Practice Mindfulness Meditations

Unlike other types of meditation, being mindful doesn't require a large time commitment or a space that is quite and calm for a specific period of time. While these things will certainly help you get into the required mindset at first, eventually you will find that you can get your mindfulness on while at the gym, doing chores or even commuting to and from work. Regardless of where you do it, the basics of mindfulness mediation are always the same.

Stick with a specific time

As with any new habit, it is crucial that you create a routine around your mindfulness meditation practices for the best results. Generally speaking, you can expect it to take about 30 days for a new habit to really stick which means that you will need to commit to going hard for just four weeks before you can expect to start seeing the best results.

Unfortunately, due to its few requirements and low impact nature, it is often quite easy to push off your set mindfulness meditation time for a later than never comes, especially if they are already very busy as it stands. If you find yourself always coming up with an excuse to get out of meditating at the moment, you may find the following piece of advice particularly useful. "Practice mindfulness meditation for fifteen minutes every day unless, of course, you are extremely busy in which case you should practice for thirty minutes instead." Don't let the outside world intrude on your potential for inner peace, find a time each day that works for you and stick with it no matter what; in a month's time, you will be glad you did.

Find a quiet place

In order to reach a state of mindfulness, you are going to want to find someplace comfortable, and quiet to sit, though not so quiet and comfortable that you are tempted to fall asleep. Then, all you need to do is breathe deeply, in and out.

BREATHE

Start by doing your best to calm your mind by taking a few deep breaths and then announce your intentions aloud to make them more tangible. From there, take several more, deep breaths and focus on the sensations that your senses are providing you as you do so. Consider how your lungs feel as they expand and the smells this action brings to your attention. If you are sitting, consider the feel of the chair on your skin, the temperature of the room and the movement of any wind across your skin. Let the sensations flow from one to another, working their way down your body completely.

Continue breathing deeply but keep your eyes and ears alert and providing you with more information than you previously thought possible. Focus on this information to the exclusion of everything else. You will likely find it difficult to shut out the constant flow of information that is running through your mind relating to things you need to do, regrets over past actions and plans that must be made, but this is completely normal. If you find your focus drifting away from the moment, take note of the mistake and move on. There is nothing to be gained from beating yourself up over it and you will only take yourself out of the moment even more.

VISUALIZE

Once you have reached a relaxed state, to remove the excess thoughts that are likely running through your head, all you need to do is picture them as a stream of bubbles that are rushing by in front of your eyes. Simply take a step back and let the thoughts flow past you without interacting with them. If one of them catches your attention and draws you into more complex thought, simply disengage and let it go. Don't focus on the fact that you were thinking about it, because that will just draw you out of the moment, simply remain in that state for as long as possible. Eventually, this will help with negative thoughts you experience in the real world as well.

In fact, with enough time and practice, you will likely find that you are able to maintain a mild meditative state even when you are otherwise focused on the world around you. This is known as a state of mindfulness and it should be the end goal of everyone who is new to the meditative practice. Being mindful means always being connected to a calming and soothing mental state as well as one that is full of joy and peace which benefits not just yourself but everyone around you.

Ignore those pesky judgments

Mindfulness is not necessarily quieting the mind or finding an eternal state of calmness. The goal here is simple. You want to pay attention to the moment you are in without judging it. When you judge a thought or something you may have done in the past, you likely, tend to dwell on it. That isn't living in the moment and is not conducive to mindful meditation. While this is easier said than done, it is a crucial step to mindful meditation. With practice, it will be easy to achieve. Be mindful of the moment, of your senses and your surroundings.

Take notice of the times you are passing judgment while practicing mindfulness. Make note of them and move on. It is easy for your mind to get lost in thought. Mindfulness meditation is the art of bringing yourself back to the moment, over and over, as many times as it takes. Don't get discouraged. In the beginning, you will find your mind wanders a lot. Reel it back in and keep moving forward.Even if your mind does happen to wander, and it will, don't be hard on yourself. It happens. Acknowledge whatever thoughts pop up, put them to the side and get back on track.

Keep it up

When you first start practicing mindfulness meditation it is very important that you do so under the understanding that you aren't going to see any results from your hard work at first and rather need to commit to the process fully before you can start receiving any rewards. Specifically, you will need to keep in mind that it is natural for your mind to wander freely for a time before you are able to guide it to where it needs to be. To better understand the mindset that you should be striving for, you might find it useful to consider the moment of complete blankness the mind experiences once it has heard a question but before it can generate an answer.

Other ways of being mindful

Showering

While many people operate on autopilot while in the shower, you can use this opportunity to give yourself a boost of mindfulness instead. This is because the senses are already in overdrive in the shower which means it is easier to get into the moment than it may be in other situations.

Exercise

While it might seem surprising, the mental state that the body finds itself in while exercising is actually quite close to a state of mindfulness, to begin with, which means it doesn't take much to push it over the edge. To get in the zone, consider the way your body feels as each muscle exerts itself as you push it to the limit.

CHORES

The repetitive nature of most chores makes them a perfect outlet for a bit of mindfulness. To make the most of these tasks, all you need to do is clear your mind beforehand and then focus on all the sensations working through the task provides you. When you are finished, consider how much better off you are now that the chore is completed and reflect on your ability to positively affect your environment.

Social media

While making a more concentrated attempt to single-task will ultimately help you practice mindfulness more easily.

Until you decide to do away with social media distractions completely, consider using them in a mindful manner instead. The next time you find yourself looking through old photographs, use that time to really remember the moment that each photograph was taken. Strain your memory and try and recall everything you can about the situation. What were the smells, the sounds, the sights? How did you feel at the moment? Really work to try and get back to that place to the extent that you block out external stimuli.

The end result

While there are plenty of proven positive side effects of practicing mindfulness, most of them are difficult to track on your own without specialized equipment as they occur at a physical level you can't see or occur on a mental level which is difficult to observe without bias. Instead, you will likely know that you are on the right track when you start to see changes to the mental conditioning you have been living with your entire life.

Modern society often instills in individuals a desire to hide their flaws and to treat any uncomfortable feelings or thoughts they have in much the same way. Over time, this leads to a desire to revise the truth and rewrite history, so it shows things in a more positive light overall. Despite not being an especially healthy way to deal with existing issues, this common habit actually stems from the well-known flight or fight reflex that helped humanity's ancestors survive against threats regardless if they were real or imagined.

While this impulse helped your ancient ancestors survive, and even thrive, amongst the harsh conditions they lived with day to day, these days, if left unchecked, it can instead easily lead to a scenario where it undermines the qualities and traits that make you unique. This, in turn, leads us to one of the greatest benefits of mindfulness. It provides those who practice it with a greater understanding of themselves which is the first step to a greater acceptance of their strengths and weaknesses and the ways the two can be used together for the best results.

Regularly practicing mindfulness, and sticking with it in the long-term, can replace this negative mindset with one that is much more positive which is referred to as radical acceptance. Simply put, radical acceptance allows you to more easily get in touch with the things you are experiencing or feeling in the moment, without having to worry about societal filters getting in the way.

Chapter 6: More Mindful Meditation Techniques

In addition to the breathing meditation, there are additional techniques that will help you enhance your awareness and become more mindful. So much is going on around us at all times, yet most of the time, we move through the day on autopilot. These exercises are designed to strengthen you mind, in the same way push-ups are meant to strengthen your body. They are also fun and will make your day more enjoyable and alive.

Focus on a Specific Object Meditation

You'll be keeping your eyes open for this meditation. The exercise is enormously helpful in preventing your focus from wandering.

Start by choosing an object. It can be anything – a flower, a picture, an interesting design, a candle … anything that touches your fancy. It should be the right size for you to observe it easily in its entirety. The purpose of the object is to be your focal point when your attention strays.

Start by closing your eyes and focusing on your breathing for 5 minutes to become relaxed.

When you feel ready, open your eyes and observe the chosen object. Notice any lights and shadows falling on the object.

Notice the texture. Is it smooth, bumpy, silky? Imagine what it would feel to the touch.

Notice the different shades of color.

Keep breathing slowly. Make no judgments about the object. You're simply an observer.

Continue as long as you wish. Ten minutes is a good time. If your mind wanders, let your awareness return to the object.

Since modern life can assault our senses on a daily basis, we can remain oblivious to the beauty around us. How often do we really notice our surroundings? This quiet exercise is helpful in keeping your focus sharp.

Body Scan Meditation

This mindful meditation is useful in releasing tension at the end of a day and in helping you fall asleep easily. Tension can frequently settle in specific areas of the body, such as shoulders, bringing on aches and fatigue. This will draw attention to trouble spots and help you relax.

Sit or lay anywhere you are comfortable. Close your eyes and breathe in and out for 5 minutes to enhance relaxation.

Shift your focus to your body.

As you breathe, become aware of various body parts. Start with the toes and feet. Move to the ankles and up the legs. As you notice any tension, breathe into it, then exhale.

Keep breathing as your awareness moves past your hips to your torso. Breathe into any tension that you may notice.

Keep breathing and notice your arms, hands and fingers. Continue to breathe into spots that feel tense.

As you continue to breathe, move your awareness to your shoulders, neck, face, and skull. Breathe slowly into any tension spots.

Spend as much time on any tense spot as is necessary. This is a wonderful exercise to relieve tension, calm your mind and hone the way we deal with stress.

Counting Mindful Meditation

As with the other meditations, sit comfortably and practice the basic breathing meditation for five minutes to relax.

Take a deep breath and inhale.

Wait a second and exhale while counting out the number 1 in your mind.

Take another deep breath and inhale.

Wait ... and count out the number 2.

Continue doing this until you have counted to number 10.

Repeat this counting process by starting with the number 9 and going backward to 1. If at any time during this exercise you lose track of a number, start over from the beginning.

As you get better, you can increase the base number to 20, or even 30.

Find Your Happy Place Meditation

Sit comfortably and enjoy five minutes of mindful breathing meditation.

Now, imagine you are in a peaceful, beautiful place. It can be a place you've been to, or a place you imagine. Whichever, it is very relaxing and soothing. There's no place you'd rather be.

Look around and experience the sights, sounds and colors around you. Notice how your body feels. Allow yourself to become lost in the beauty of your special place. Take all the time you want.

Notice the sense of peace and calm flooding through your body. When you are ready to leave, take a deep breath and open your eyes. You are now ready to face the challenges of your day.

Chapter 7: Learning About Judgement

When someone says something to you and you get upset by it, what you are doing is placing judgement onto that particular thing that was said. It's natural that you do that. This is why emotional responses happen but when you practice mindfulness, you are able to switch off those automatic responses, which are very clever, because it means that you have control over your mind and do not let things change your emotional state.

The thing is that if you say someone has been unkind to you, what you actually mean is that your mind has judged that they have been unkind to you. Your mind makes judgments all the time. Every time that it does this, it jumps out of the moment and into this awful stage where emotions kick in. Thus, if you could skip the judgement stage, you wouldn't feel so bad about things and you would be able to go on to the next moment in your life without having to deal with all the pressures of life. Of course, this would be in an ideal world, and we don't live in an ideal world. Thus, when you introduce mindfulness, you take a different approach to life and tend to live in the moment, letting thoughts that come to you drift away when they are not significant to the moment. This training of the mind also helps you to judge less. You are told not to judge, but to simply accept that the thoughts happened and let go of them. Imagine the power that this gives you if you can then do the same thing in real life.

What you need in order to do this is to employ something that is called empathy. Buddhist philosophy actually supports this and it's included in the Eight Fold Path of Buddhism, but let me explain how it works for you, as a beginner. If you don't let what people say to you hurt you, you open yourself up to be more understanding of their viewpoint. Thus, you know that there is a reason why that person has said something hurtful, and you look behind the words to the reason and find empathy.

You are able to see why things that were bad were said and are able to be more understanding about it. Empathy means being able to step into someone else's shoes and see things from another viewpoint.

I remember when I first used this side of mindfulness in my life. Someone said something to me that would normally upset me. Instead of being upset, I examined in my mind the reason behind someone saying something of this nature and found that the person who spoke was a very sad person with a lot of family problems. Insults actually say a lot more about the person speaking them than the person having to listen to them. I then opened up a dialog with this person and was able to see things from his point of view. When you can do that and be in the moment, you lose all will to use negative things such as revenge, anger, frustration or jealousy and are able to sidestep those negative influences in a very effective way.

The first thing that people think of when they face negative thoughts is indeed to rebound that negativity. However, mindfulness means that you become mindful of your own approach to things and are better able to stay calm and in the moment. I actually used this argument on children and found that they were better able to get on with people when they understood that bad things said don't always mean what they initially think they do. My children are very compassionate children because they have learned mindfulness and know that negative response or holding grudges does them no good at all, whereas being more understanding and taking positivity from one moment to the next helps them to remain calmer and be better friends to those other kids who are going through similar situations.

Mindfulness means being ever present, but it also means being ever aware that the world around us is changing. What you feel one moment, you may not feel the next and that doesn't just work with bad things. It also means that you need to be more present to accept and enjoy all the good things that the world is offering you. If you have ever had something really embarrassing happen to you, at the time it happens, you think it's the end of the world. It isn't of course, and within a week, you may be laughing at the situation, but when you start to think in a mindful way, it's this very moment that is all that matters. Anger will pass, negativity will pass, insults will pass and the next moment may offer something entirely different. It is your job to observe these changes and to embrace each moment with all of the compassion you can so that you make the most of the moments you have and are ready to move onto the next moment, taking all that positivity with you.

Thus, judgement isn't something you should indulge in. If asked for an opinion, by all means give one, but be mindful in your reply. Remember that all things are transient. Life itself is transient and will pass. If you can keep your heart happy by not passing judgement on those around you, you will find that you are almost immune to others passing judgement on you because you are aware of the transient nature of life but also aware that it is the judgement part of your reaction that dictates how negative a situation becomes. If you refuse to judge, but are happy to be yourself and to go through life one moment at a time, you find that you make more friends, you have less worries and you enjoy life a lot more.

Chapter 8: Control Fear

We fear a deadlock work. We fear a low pay in the field we're going to seek after. We fear to lose a friend or family member. We fear a business atmosphere loaded with turbulence, change, and disturbance. We fear an existence without significance. People fear being disappointed. What fear does is that it drains life from of us. It doesn't have to be balanced nor does it have to be valid to make one anxious. Often when powered by an over-thinking personality that is stuck in an endless loop, fear will keep us up the night and weakens amid the day. Something as little as a whisper can trigger its passionate chokehold. We pass by the TV and see news cut of the disorder in the center east. We discover a site with a story of somebody confronting a troublesome well-being circumstance. We hear individuals say how terrible business is 'these days'.

By lights out, we are charmed in an undeniable war with our psyche battling the stories it invokes. Will I fall sick? Will I lose my employment? Will I have enough cash? Is the wrongdoing rate going up? Will I ever reach somebody? Will I rest this evening? Will I survive? These are all categorized as fear of the future.

Comprehend what fear is and what it isn't Fear is a feeling. What's more much the same as other feelings, for example, love, displeasure or bliss, fear is something we can take care of. It is something that we can succeed. All the more significantly we must overcome fear. Otherwise, it will incapacitate us.

On the off chance that we can't break free from it, fear can obliterate our soul.

Quit nourishing the fear

We latently expend a large number of messages a day. We should quit permitting others to nourish the fear setting aside the 10 o'clock news, contrary individuals and perusing into what may happen in the future. Forbid the pessimism from entering the sanctuary of your centered and dynamic personality.

Supplant the 'stress trigger' with something more helpful

Be proactive at what goes into our brain every day, particularly in the morning when our psyche is generally fresh. Here are four approaches to kick start the day. Perused a book, listen to an elevating melody, watch a movie feature on YouTube, say a mantra or an insistence.

Companions help to overcome fear when they lift you up and never cut you down

Associations with companions serve to feed us particularly when we require support. Whether we're at the place of love or at the wearing occasion or at the Labor Day BBQ, encompassing ourselves with delight, fun, and support from companions can help us understand that our fear is lost. We can easily overcome the fear of the future while we converse with our companions.

Have you been having trouble overcoming fear? That's cool, it's normal, and everyone goes through it at some point. Fear is one of the strongest forces in the world. Sometimes it can get the particularly debilitating thought and can hinder you from really accomplishing great things in life. Finding a way to control your fears will not only make you healthier, but happier as well.

So that said, here are four ways you can begin overcoming your fear right now;

Try some meditation. If you can take 15 minutes a day to just relax and focus on yourself, the effect is incredible. Doing this will allow you to put things in perspective, and ultimately realize there's nothing to be afraid of.

Write down All of Your Fears. Do this and then categorize them. They should all fall easily into 4-6 categories which are the underlying uncertainties. Now you've gone from dozens of fears to a few. Much easier to tackle.

Do something fun. Have a tough decision you need to make and you're afraid of how to go about it? Go do something fun to help you put things in perspective. When your mind is clear again, it will be much easier to make the right decision.

Find a friend and talk to them. Most of us tend to keep many things bottled up for so long it drives us crazy. Find someone who you're comfortable with, who ideally has gone through a similar situation as you. You'll be glad to get your thoughts off your chest, and they may be able to add some valuable insight.

If you spent as much time focused on believing in a good outcome, having faith that everything is going to work out, knowing that no matter what happens you will survive and be stronger for it, you could alleviate the burden of stress and anxiety that worry is wrapped in.

Worrying can not only affect your mood and your attitude towards life but it can take a toll on your health as well. You may think that worrying is a safety net and it will protect you from some unforeseen misfortune but since you can't predict the future; why try?

If you absolutely can't shake the worry habitat, at least try and think of both outcomes. Instead of filtering everything through the oh-no-what-if-this-happens viewpoint which has a negative spin attached to it, think about having a positive outcome too.

You should be concerned about some things which you take the appropriate steps in implementing the necessary changes toward your desired outcome. But on the other hand, some things are out of your control and you have to do your best and then forget the rest!

When you are struggling with control and worry remember the Serenity Prayer: God/Allah/Higher Power grant me the serenity to accept the things I cannot change; the courage to change the things I can; and the wisdom to know the difference.

Just for today, clear your list. Remove all the "what if's" and just breathe. If you insist on worrying, schedule a time to worry, give yourself 15 minutes and then let it go and enjoy the day. There are no guarantees in life and we deal with life a day at a time and sometimes a minute at a time.

If you spend all of your time in worry-land you miss out on being present right here, right now. You fill your mind with fears and doubts and you may be telling yourself stories that may never come true. So shed the dread and know that everything is working out for your good.

Chapter 9: Mindlessness Versus Mindfulness

Generally, all people have five senses: seeing, hearing, speaking, touching and tasting. When you make the old new again, you are actually awakening your sense of sight. When you are being attentive to what other people say, you are awakening your sense of hearing.

Waking up your sense of speaking is achieved after you observe your thoughts. How often have you observed that you sometimes mean something yet say another thing? Being mindful of your speech means you have attained a certain degree of empathy.

If you can place yourself in the shoes of the person you are talking with, you will probably have an idea of how he interprets or take the words you say. Being tactless is a proof of mindlessness. This is the opposite of being mindful which means that a tactless person is not within the present moment.

Every now and then, it is easier to understand a lot in terms of what it is in contrast or is not. So, here are some other situations that show mindlessness:

Accidents arising from carelessness, daydreaming or negligence

A perfect example is when a house gets burned down because the people inside the house slept without putting out a lighted candle during an evening when a power failure occurred. Had they been mindful, they would have considered this, though their thoughts were elsewhere and not in the moment they needed to be in.

Awkwardness

An example scenario is when a person highly valued comes dropping by your home unannounced and you end up fidgeting and make them feel uncomfortable. A mindful person is always ready to welcome whatever the moment may bring and whether that's unexpected visitors, a storm or a wonderfully sunny day, a mindful person will not be phased by what is happening.

Breaking things

This is common to teenagers who are so engrossed with their math assignments that they unknowingly break their pencil or a glass of whatever while reaching out to it without even bothering to see where their hands are going. If you break things because of thoughtlessness, this is indeed mindless. You are not paying attention to the moment and thus make mistakes. You may be doing one job while trying to do another. Multi-tasking people often make mistakes because they are not giving their whole mind to either one or other of the jobs that they are undertaking.

Dropping things

Typical scenario for this is when you drop your house key while attempting to insert it in the keyhole.This happens when the attempt is made to open the door while both your hands are carrying things, such as your purse in one hand and a bag of grocery items on the other hand. A mindful person would place the shopping safely at his/her feet before trying to open the door, being ever mindful that the load may impede opening the door.

Failing to see subtle feelings of bodily discomfort, hurt, tension or fatigue of another person

This is common in a group activity when the leader keeps shouting orders to his members all day through without even minding if the previous order had already been completed or not. This form of insensitivity is not mindful of the pain of others. Mindful people are empathetic and thus can see the world from where the other person is sitting.

Not remembering a name as soon as it is spoken

Can you recall an instance when someone was introduced to you and you end up asking for his name again even when it was just spoken to you? The problem here is that you were not mindful during the introduction to that person and did not give them the moment of your time it took to become acquainted.

Listening to someone talking to you while your other ear is listening to something else

You see this quite often, I am sure. Or you may even be one of those people to talk to someone while listening to music through your earphones. Mindful people do one or the other. They listen to a friend or they listen to music because both merit the same amount of respect.

Getting so concentrated on goals that you forget what you are doing for the moment

This frequently happens to almost everyone and in a variety of ways. One example though is when you rush a child to the hospital. And while there, your mind is reminding you that you have a series of deadlines to meet. Hence, instead of attending to the sick child's needs, you end up worrying about your deadlines. A mindful person is able to get the priorities right and be present in that moment when the child is in need of him/her.

Getting occupied in your thoughts and emotions

There are many scenarios for this case.I am pretty sure you have seen, heard and may even have been asked by someone this question: "A penny for your thoughts?"The problem is that when you are self-absorbed, you are not able to take in the moment that you are in because you are too busy to notice it.

Being worried by yesterday's decisions and tomorrow's challenges

Many, if not all, of us make mistakes in the many decisions or choices we make each day.When one cannot move on past a mistake or keeps worrying about the possibility of making another mistake in the future, that person is definitely not living in the moment. Someone who practices mindfulness would be able to prioritize and to make the best attempt possible in that moment in time regardless of past experience.

Not being aware of what he is doing

This is easily manifested in eating or doing manual work.In eating, people oftentimes eat in a rush that they even forget to taste the food they eat.Another is when a person does manual chores like watering the plants or merely sweeping the floor.

Though they perform such tasks, their thoughts are really somewhere else.It is like flying a plane put on autopilot.Hence, some take forever to finish a task on hand.And what it makes it funnier is when you experience difficulty recalling the details of what happened!

Responding emotionally in particular ways

This is not easy to witness but it happens.Personally, I experienced this while riding a bus back home from work late in the evening of a Sunday.I felt so tired and was surprised to find tears running down my cheeks.It was a weird feeling that an intense emotion can just come out in the open from the depths of my thoughts. There can be other instances that show mindlessness as well. From daydreaming, rationalizing when performing chores, to multitasking, mindlessness is in command. If you act in any of the cited instances at times, then you are a normal constituent of today's humanity.

The quotation below sums up mindfulness as opposed to mindlessness. Mindfulness makes you present in the moment in time and makes you a very valuable part of that moment, whereas mindlessness may mean that you are passing moments that have very little meaning or substance.

Why? The reason is simple. If you are not present in that moment, how can you benefit from it?

Being present does indeed change you. You take more time with decisions. You know where you are and you also know the value of the moment that you are in. It not only changes your character – but it changes the whole structure of your values and that's exceedingly important if you want to embrace your life and make the most of it. Tomorrow, you may be dead. Tomorrow, you may be something of the past. Thus, to ensure that you make the most of the life that you have, mindfulness is the way forward.

Chapter 10: Mindfulness Meditation

Mindfulness meditation is not complicated, but it should be practiced carefully. By no means should you just do the techniques you will learn automatically, as if they were part of a routine program that you engage in out of obligation. With that being said, mindfulness meditation goes hand in hand with a state of increased awareness and awakening that allows for no superficiality. Remember that mindfulness teaches you how to escape any suffering or discomfort that may tinge your life.

The easiest form of mindfulness is achieved by means of sitting meditation. You surely know the classic position in which Buddha is depicted. You are definitely not trying to imitate Buddha when practicing mindfulness, but attempting to find yourself and appreciate every moment of your own life. However, there was much wisdom in Buddha's words and you should at least remember his words of wisdom: our source of suffering is running away from direct experience. Starting from his notion of absolute acceptance and harmony with the self and the universe, you can practice mindfulness by paying attention to each detail of experience as it arises in a completely non-judgmental way.

The following meditation techniques are quite simple for beginners and they focus on your body, your breath, and your thoughts. First of all, you should try to situate your body in a good setting for meditation. If you can afford having an entire room that is incredibly quiet and relaxing, filled with optimal light and color and allowing for no disturbance or disharmony, that is great. However most of us cannot and it's easier to just find a corner of a 'normal' room where you arrange something like a small altar for this activity. Ideally, you should decorate that corner or room with pictures and objects that have sacred meanings to you one way or another. Make sure no distractions are around, only calming and/or subtly inspiring images on the walls. The best way to take care of this aspect is getting rid of the usual 'food for thought' that actually keeps you farther away from mindfulness: TV set, computer, internet etc. During mindfulness meditation, you are supposed to get into the deepest communication with yourself and with your natural thoughts and sensations.

As for the place you should use for sitting, you can use a comfortable chair or you can sit directly on the floor on a soft cushion or on a blanket, for instance. Ideally, a more direct contact with 'the ground' is desirable. However, if for any objective reason you would be uncomfortable sitting on the floor, you are of course free to sit on a chair or a bench, as that is not necessarily going to affect your meditation. What you should be careful about is the stability of your 'meditation seat': it shouldn't wiggle or produce you any pressure/discomfort. Cross your legs in front of you and place your hands on your thighs or knees with palms facing downwards. Look gently in front of you, letting your gaze linger on the objects that you can find around. Don't try to focus too sharply; the idea is letting your eyes rest as naturally as possible on whatever is surrounding you. It doesn't really have to be anything special: if you're facing your window, just look at the forms and contours of the clouds; if you're facing vegetation, let your senses revel in the colors and shapes; if you see houses in front of you, just move your gaze gently over the objects without straying into what is not there (e.g. don't try to imagine what is inside or people who may inhabit them, only focus on what is visible to the eyes); if you have your walls in front of you, looks softly at the pictures you have on them etc.

The next thing you have to do is keep your back straight, but relaxed. Let your front be open and gently hold your stare on what you can see in front of you for a few minutes in a row. If your mind wanders, gently take note of the concrete features of the objects in front of you: remind yourself to come back in the present moment, right in the setting you are located in. Nevertheless, you shouldn't do this in a too forced way: don't judge yourself harshly for thinking about something else, don't reprimand yourself explicitly or indirectly by dwelling on any negative energy. Simply bring your thoughts back to what you can see and observe in front of you and try to notice as many details as you can about your environment. Remember: after all, mindfulness means experiencing the present moment to the fullest with your whole mind. It is not any kind of multi-directionality or divergence that will help you feel fulfilled and in harmony with the concrete world around you.

After you have taken in your environment for a few minutes (about 5 minutes would be ideal), you can now focus on your breath. Notice the rhythm of your natural breath without trying to change it. Just make sure you are extremely aware of the 'movements' of your own breath: inhale, exhale; do this in a conscious and attentive way for a few minutes, as if being one with your own breath, playing its very tune with your conscious mind in perfect harmony. Try to follow the stream of your breath as the air flows into your body and your lungs and as it leaves your body afterwards. Focus mentally on your breath as if it were a traceable fine thread that you can follow with your thoughts.

After you made sure you are in touch with your breath, try focusing on your body and any sensations you might experience. How does the pillow or blanket beneath you feel? Are you barefoot? Do you feel any cold or warm air? What are you wearing? How do your clothes feel? When your palms touch your thighs, what precise tactile impressions do you get? Can you sense any smell in your room? Ideally, you should burn some incense or candles in order to stimulate your senses. Can you feel any taste in your mouth? Perhaps you have just eaten something delicious and you can still vaguely perceive the taste? In any case don't imagine anything, don't force yourself to create mentally what is not already in front of you and in you. Remember: if you can feel it in your body and you can take it in via your 5 senses, it is real.

The next step is focusing on your thoughts. The bottom line is that having your thoughts wander and develop in a stream of consciousness on their own is a natural mental process and you should accept it and treat it with tolerance without letting yourself be controlled or absorbed by it. The point is to become aware of this process and be the master over it. How can you do this? It's easy: just pay attention to the direction of your thoughts during your meditation exercise. If you think about the last film you watched, slowly push it out of your mind, since it belongs in the past. If you find yourself fantasizing about a vacation or your crush, bring your thoughts back to yourself gently and focus on what is in front of you in the present moment. The easiest way to do this is to bring your thoughts from an immaterial reality at first to your breath. Once you 'caught' yourself dreaming of something unreal or lingering on the past, follow the flow of your breath naturally for a few minutes. This simple act will bring you back to your immediate reality, back into your sensations and physical environment.

This meditation exercise should be practiced for 10-15 minutes for starters. After you have learned how to gently control your thoughts and your mind (think the strategy 'an iron hand in a silk glove' for this purpose), you are already an expert in mindful meditation. This means you shouldn't let yourself grow too used to what you can easily do. Instead you should increase the duration of your exercise to 20-30 minutes. Eventually this calming and nourishing mindfulness exercise can extend up to 45 minutes. You will be able to decide on this aspect once you realize how beneficial and revitalizing it is.

The key to mindfulness meditation is getting a grip over your own thoughts and being able to 'maneuver' yourself back into the delights of the present moment instead of longing for unreal worlds. There may be a preconception that mindfulness meditation could imply voiding your mind of your usual thought tracks and patterns, of your memories, etc. This couldn't be further from the truth. The goal of this practice is exercising control over your own thoughts and avoiding stress or pain. When you are regularly swept away from the present into a fantasy world or into recollections of past events, something may be wrong – are you really satisfied with what you already have? Are you even aware of what is tangible to you and graspable in front of you? Most of the time when we neglect the joys of the present moment, we do it unknowingly, because we may miss something or we simply lack practice. Through mindfulness meditation, you are actually intentionally training your mind via your own will.

Chapter 11: Eleven Buddhist Techniques For Mindfulness

Practicing the art of mindfulness is facilitating your mind to think about things and aspects that you choose. Learning to live in the present moment is focusing on things that are happening in the moment. When you master mindfulness, you learn to observe and see the happenings around the world without judgment.

Emotions are an imperative part of mindfulness and you cannot ignore them at all. However, it is very important that you learn to let go of these emotions.

Technique # 15 – Be aware of what your mind is focusing on – Do not allow yourself to think about things you don't want to. You have to consciously work so that your mind focuses on things that you want it to focus on.

It is extremely easy to get completely wrapped up in your emotions thinking of various incidents that occurred during the day including those that happened in your personal relationships and also those that happened at work. Practice your mind to focus only on those things that you choose.

You should start by focusing your mind on objects and things in the outside world. And once you get better at this, start focusing on things happening inside you.

Be watchful of your mind wandering away; gently pull it back to that one thing you choose to focus on each time.

Technique # 16 – Watch your actions mindfully – There is a vast difference between knowing what you are doing and being mindful of what you are doing. When you are talking to a friend, you KNOW you are talking to him or her; that is an autopilot mode. But are you MINDFUL of how and what you are talking? Pay close attention to each detail of your actions.

Technique # 17 – Be aware of the purpose of your actions – When you pay attention to details, when you are focused in the present moment; these are ways of being aware of the purpose of your actions.

Pay close attention to what you are thinking; pay close attention to whether what you are thinking is the same as what you are doing; this will help you identify the purpose of your action.

For every action you do, focus on the feelings involved; focus on the minute details of the action, and focus your mind on the present moment.

Technique # 18 – Leave the past behind – How often do you look back in your life and say to yourself, "I wish I had/hadn't done that?" How often do you look back and pine away for something that happened many years ago?

Very often, isn't it? And it you noticed, going back to the past is also on autopilot. You are peeling potatoes and your mind is thinking about a sad event that happened in your past. Many times, these feelings, whether happy or sad, can bring a smile or tears unknowing to you. It is almost like an impulsive reaction.

Someone else is looking at you and asking you, "Why are you smiling or why are you crying?" Then you wake up and realize you are actually peeling potatoes, but your mind has wandered off. Endeavor to avoid this. While you really cannot control your emotions, at least be aware that your mind is traveling to a place you don't want it to. Gently bring it back to the peeling of the potato.

Technique # 19 – Do not think of the future – Planning for the future is an important aspect of our lives. "Do not think of the future" does not mean do not plan prudently. It only means that you should not get so caught up with your future that the fears and anxiety with something that may or may not happen tomorrow would affect your state of mind right now.

Planning your future is also an act of the present. Make a to-do list for tomorrow. Focus on making the list to ensure you have noted everything you can think of. Now, put that list away and pick up the to-do list of today. From that pick up the first task and focus your mind and body on doing and completely that task to the best of your abilities.

Technique # 20 – Avoid looking at your watch – It is a very common and unwitting task that we keep repeating ever so often. We keep looking at our watch to keep track of time. We are checking it even when there is nothing to do. Remember you have no control over time. Whether you do something or you don't do something, time will pass; so don't waste time hassling over time.

Checking the time is fine as long as you do worry yourself about how slowly or how fast the time is passing by. That is your mind working. If you have work to do, do it and be in the present moment. If you do not have work to do, then sit back and relax and even then be in the present moment.

Technique # 21 – Take time off to do nothing at all – Productivity is great, but doing nothing is important too. Take some time off regularly to sit back and do nothing but watch the world go by. By doing nothing, I mean nothing! Don't look at your smartphone; don't watch TV; don't watch a movie; don't read a book; don't eat; don't drink; don't walk; don't run; don't talk; don't do anything; just sit by the window side or any other favorite place of yours and let yourself be!

While you do nothing, you are truly experiencing living and enjoying the world around you. Watch the bird fly by; watch the leaves in the tree rustle; watch the bus going down the road; watch the dog walking contently; watch the waves dashing against the rocks; feel the breeze against your face; feel the ground beneath your feet; feel the warmth of the sun; hear the sound of rustling leaves; hear the sound of a vehicle going by; hear the bark of the dog; hear the laughter of someone nearby; hear the tapping of someone's feet nearby; do nothing but watch, feel, hear, and enjoy everything around you.

Of course, your thoughts will go away somewhere else. Cajole them back to the present moment and observe everything around you. You don't need to record anything - just sit back and do nothing.

Technique # 22 – Do not be judgmental and avoid negativity – When you are in the present moment and living in the moment, enjoy the things around you without passing judgment. Observe the surrounding sights, sounds and smells without passing any kind of judgment. If you smell something that you don't seem like; simply smell and don't pass judgment. If you see something that you like; again just watch and don't pass judgment.

Instead of blaming anyone, see if you can empathize with the person or situation. When you judge something or someone, remember that you are actually predicting the outcome of a present moment and this is not based on anything really true but is based on someone's behavior and your view of it. Just be objective about everything happening around you.

Negativity saps energy, which is already such a limited resource for us. Avoid negative thoughts, ideas, or emotions to the best possible extent.

Technique # 23 – Do not hold on to any emotions; good or bad – Being mindful does not mean being thrilled or excited always. It means letting go of all emotions as much as possible. When you live in the present moment without judgment or without comparing it to something in the past or something that you envision in the future, you will have the power to see and appreciate the positivity around you.

Technique # 24 – Treat your emotions and feelings like how you would treat the weather – Mindfulness means living fully in the present moment without expectations, without fears, without anxieties, etc. However, living a life of mindfulness does not mean stoicism. Embrace your happy emotions, but remember to let them go.

Emotions rise and fade! Let them rise and let them fade. You cannot hold on to them. You cannot control emotions just like you cannot control the weather. If you are thinking that you will control emotions in such a way that you will keep happiness and give away sadness, then you are not living in the present moment. Mindfulness is living in the moment and letting everything else including emotions go.

Technique # 25 – Treat everyone with compassion and kindness – The core of mindful living is compassion and kindness for all around you. As you live your daily life, you are bound to meet people who will think differently from the way you do. You will encounter people who are seemingly better off than you and/or worse off than you. As a practitioner of mindfulness, you must treat everyone with compassion and kindness.

The choice of practicing mindfulness is your personal choice and your personal journey. Letting go of your judgmental attitude is a choice you made and this non-judgmental attitude should be even for those people who choose not to practice mindfulness.

Chapter 12: Why Do You Need It In Your Life?

If we were to pin point a natural or average state for humans it would be discontent and dissatisfaction. Even when we have apparently everything from the outside-a house with a garden, a fancy car, an attractive spouse-The American Dream, we still find ourselves wishing for more and wanting something way above and beyond what we have achieved.

It is not just about materialistic desires but rather everything that our heart calls for- friends to boast about, a love like that in the movies. It is perpetual effort to be more than what we are and have more than what we have. Life has turned into a constant struggle.

Studies and surveys shows that crime rate is on a constant rise. More so in the metropolitans as opposed to the suburbs. Newspapers and television reports are filled with incidents of violent and horrific felonies. This is not in some place with the laws of jungle where humans have to steal to eat and kill to survive but rather in our nations that are supposedly the light bearers of civilization. Why is there no seeming end to these offences?

Dissatisfaction is the answer. The more we are progressing, the more discontent we are of our lives. The more we gain, the more we want.

There is a constant undercurrent of negative energy within all of us. It sometimes erupts out like a volcano. In war, in sports and within the workplace. We are all on the lookout for an excuse to tear each other out. This bestiality is hidden behind a facade of manners and etiquettes. We might have moved past the ways of Rome where the whole city would turn out to watch the spectacle of death. Though today we look down upon it, we still very much desire competition and fights to the death.

It is only the rules of the game that have changed. The game is still very much alive. We find such morose pleasure in other's defeats. We look down upon our subordinates at work. We leave no stone unturned in ensuring that someone else doesn't climb up the ladder. Worldly success is not just about doing your own thing. It is about killing all the opponents to be the lone survivor in the arena. We would still kill to watch a show at the Coliseum. The only thing that has changed is that it is a different kind of show.

Once we have won the trophy, the golden sword, the crown or the kingdom, then begins another constant struggle to hold onto that position. We are not just content with achieving something but we also want to hold it close to our hearts, within our souls forever and ever.

We are so obsessed with never letting go that we cannot even accept that our bodies are deteriorating. That they will age and that we too come with an expiry date. Just take a look at the cosmetic industry to get an idea about what I mean. Reverse the process of aging, serums for early signs of aging, surgical procedures to reclaim the lost glow. We are incapable of letting of any glory that we might once have had. Even if that glory was a gift from Mother Nature and we had no part in achieving it.

Such pride is taken in family heirlooms and family traditions. Ever heard an aristocrat talk about his family history? He can go on for hours about the feats of his ancestors. How they were the smartest, bravest and the richest people on the planet during their time.
The same mentality is reflected in Nations. They are all in the trance of what they once were. Never letting go of the past hence never really living the future. Whole generations pass by that do not live their lives in the current moment.

Such is the comparison between the exaggerated glories of the past and the mundane nature of the present that there is a constant rift of disagreement between the mind and the soul. The true soul as it is a part of the soul of the universe knows that the life that is to be lived is passing right in front of our eyes, but the mind is too rigid with the impressions that it has gained.

Mindfulness is the answer to this perpetual agony of discontent. Achievement of perfect peace can liberate us from the naked ambition of all other achievements. Awareness of the world around us will make us aware that all we desire is not needed.

Chapter 13: The Power Of Yoga

Yoga is becoming more popular around the world due to its long-term health benefits. Not only can it keep a person feeling lean and flexible, it also has benefits for the mind and spirit. Many people practice yoga and are willing to do anything to get their morning fix in, just because of the way it makes them feel afterward. It has been said that yoga opens the mind, cleanses the body, and awakens the soul. Have you ever watched a group of people leaving a yoga class? There is a sense of peace and tranquility about them.

How to include Yoga in every day life

Doing yoga just a few times a week can have benefited you with your mindfulness. Keeping the channel open to the Universe is definitely more likely if you practice using the breath and moving the body in ways that release that trapped energy.

How can Yoga help us become Mindful?

There are many different types of yoga. Some yoga exercises are known to release old stagnant energy from the body and releasing blockages. When we release these blockages we become more aware of our mind, body, and soul. When we are more aware, we live a life that corresponds to this, causing people to break free from the mundaneness of life and living out their days in a more fulfilling manner.

Morning Yoga

Starting the day with some morning stretches is not only a good way to start the day, it is also a good way to stretch the body after it has been resting for several hours. Many people decide to work with the sunrise which is known to keep them grounded. When we work with the cycle of the sun it can help us to stay grounded as we are connecting to nature and the cycle of life itself.

Stretching correctly to release Energy

We all get blockages within the body which can be caused by many things such as negative energy, holding onto the past, and even eating foods that the body can't handle over a long amount of time. By stretching the body in certain ways, especially in ways that the body doesn't take on every day, can help to push out these blockages over time. Yoga, such as Kundalini yoga, is specifically targeted to take the energy that we carry in the lower part of the spine and push it upwards. After time, this can leave a person feeling like they have more energy and even that they are more connected to the people around them.

Chakra Aligning

We all have seven main chakras within us. Starting from the base, these consist of the following:

Root Chakra

Sacral Chakra

Solar Plexus Chakra

Heart Chakra

Throat Chakra

Third Eye Chakra

Crown Chakra

Each chakra holds a different power but if one is just a little out of balance it causes other chakras to over work themselves leaving a person feeling agitated, lethargic, disconnected, and even depressed. Yoga is a way to align all seven chakras and keep them working at their fullest. As each chakra is based in a specific part of the body, doing particular yoga exercises can awaken it and get it moving again. This is another reason why yoga has become so popular because, even if the person practicing doesn't realize what is happening, they are getting their chakras moving and creating a healthy balance within their lives.

Simple Tips:

·When you awake in the morning, stand tall, arms above your head and stretch the body, allowing the energy to flow through your spine

·Find a friend to do a yoga class with once a week

·Make friends with the instructor so that you'll feel more comfortable in the class

·Find the appropriate crystal for each Chakra and place them on you whilst meditating

·If a Chakra is out of balance, find the right crystal and keep in in your pocket

·If a Chakra is underactive, wear the color of it today or eat foods of the same color.

Chapter 14: Why Practice Mindfulness?

Physical health, mental health, stress reduction, mood improvement, better sleep, better eating, better relationships... the list can go on for as long as another 5WH book! There have been numerous studies on mindfulness and each of them shows benefits to several areas of people's lives. The above are some of the most pertinent improvements that can be had. There are many more.

Some people ask "why would I do mindfulness? What I already do is..." this or that. I often respond to them by saying rather jokingly "why wouldn't you mindfulness?" This is an exercise in awareness of anything and everything that we do. If a person says the best way of reducing their anxiety is by getting on their motorcycle riding as hard as they can, this is a moment where they can practice mindfulness and, in some way, are already doing so. This may surprise some people because when we are doing things like hobbies that keep us preoccupied, it does not seem as if we are the aware or focused until you realize that what you are doing requires you to focus your attention. In that moment, mindfulness becomes apparent in most activities that we do to help us relax, stay calm, or reduce stress. The man who rides the motorcycle to reduce stress is probably not thinking about his work day while he rides, and he is not thinking about the house payment due the next day, but rather is enjoying the smells, the sites, and sensations of riding his motorcycle. On the other end the spectrum is the person who does scrapbooking or arts and crafts after getting home from a long day of work. This person is probably focused more on cutting a piece of paper to resemble butterfly instead of thinking about how insulting their boss was that day or thinking about how annoying their at coworkers are, and in that moment they are fully conscious of what they are doing. This truly is a level of mindfulness, and in reality, the act of doing these things mindfully could potentially increase the joy and value of doing them. I sometimes use an example from my life when I was working at an adolescent mental health facility where up to 240 children, all with severe mental health issues, were house together. This could be one of the most stressful environments a person can experience and I recall an event of trying to keep one child from attacking another. If I had been worried about the outcome, worried about what was going to happen next, I would have become anxious and upset or angry about the situation. Instead, I asked the teen what he needed and he told me he wanted something to drink. As I obliged, he calmed down. Another great example is a person who drives to work and is so caught up in thinking about what they have to do that day, the person may arrive at work having driven 30 miles and not even realize how they got there. Maybe you have had this experience as well? If this person instead notices all the experiences of driving to work, they are in the present moment when they arrive at the destination and are no longer stressed. Instead, they simply are in the moment and if they can maintain this level of moment to moment awareness throughout the day, things bother them less, they get over things easier, and can actually increase their productivity. That increase in mood and effectiveness is why mindfulness can be so helpful. Allowing ourselves the opportunity to be present in the moment is one of the greatest gifts we can give to ourselves.

Not being able to know what the future holds or focusing on the past and being afraid to repeat keeps us from ever being able to grow or change, but if we can focus on the present moment we start a notice that we may even care and love ourselves simply for being who we are. The practice of mindfulness is the first step toward loving yourself, but also the path to better understanding others. This results in being more compassionate, open, and caring with others and ultimately being able to enjoy your life and the people in it. Without mindfulness we are left mindless, and in that state we're no better than zombies.

Chapter 15: Learning To Be Less Judgmental

Mindfulness techniques for reducing stress are used all over the world. Mindfulness meditation has been proven to positively impact many different health issues and illnesses, especially those caused by stress, like depression and anxiety. One negative impact of dealing with stress on a long-term basis is that people often become hyper-vigilant. In other words, they get caught up in distorted thought loops and negative feelings that lead nowhere. As soon as you have difficulty with regulating your own feelings, you are at a risk for developing an anxiety or depression disorder. Many researchers have proven that becoming a part of a program for mindfulness will decrease the likelihood of ruminating about thoughts and reacting strongly to emotions. Skillfully learning how to use your own attention is what will teach you to be more positive toward your emotions.

Are You Born with Your Emotional Disposition?

Many believe that people are born with certain emotional dispositions, and that some are inherently happier than other people and that this cannot be changed by will. But one study challenged this assumption. The study looked at stressed out employees who took on mindfulness on a daily basis for two months. The result was that their moods shifted to more positive outlooks and that they changed their brain's disposition.

Mindfulness can help you pay attention to what is going on in your mind, observe your moods, and make conscious decisions that do not add to the negativity in your mind, which will often lead to depression or anxiety.

Mindfulness and Social Anxiety: Mindfulness can benefit those who suffer from social anxiety. One study found that those with this disorder saw improved depression and anxiety symptoms, along with a rise in self-esteem, after only two months of daily mindfulness and meditation. In this study, the participants were instructed to read negative beliefs about themselves repeatedly and were shown to have less of a negative emotion toward this after two months of mindfulness, because they learned how to instead focus on their breath. They were not told to change what they thought, but to allow thoughts to come on their own without fighting or adding to them.

Brain Activity Changes: This study also observed activity in the brain with those in the program, both before and after they engaged in the practice of mindfulness. The results were that the participants had far less activity happening in the fear-generating area of their brains; the amygdala. In fact, studies show that the amygdala can shrink with consistent practice of mindfulness after just two weeks.

Mindfulness Method Number Seven: Setting Aside Your Judgments:

The next method for getting better at mindfulness is to stop judging whether or not the practice you are doing is worth it or not. Rather than constantly checking in with whether or not your bad habits are changing, wait until you are well into the practice to judge that. In studies done on mindfulness practice, participants often say that they become nicer to themselves, and appreciate others and themselves more with time.

Being Kinder to Yourself: Even those who typically are very mean to themselves learn to change this by being more mindful. Clients in studies become less apprehensive toward their own emotions and thoughts. This is because they learned to sit with those thoughts and emotions and see where they lead. This causes them to react less to them and access a state of calm within themselves.

Repetition: Learning how to observe your emotions and thoughts on a repeated basis as just emotions and thoughts - without getting carried away by them - will bring you some much needed freedom. That is why so many people consider mindfulness a life changing habit to acquire.

Mindfulness Method Number Eight: Challenge Yourself.

In order to stay interested in mindfulness, you should find ways to challenge yourself and keep the process interesting. Here are some ideas for doing that:

Read Philosophy: Some feel much more engaged in a practice of mindfulness when they supplement their path with reading philosophy. This can help them feel more in touch with themselves and the universe.

Stay Honest: Every time you meditate, see it as a chance to discover and beat resistance you have about seeing yourself clearly. Be honest about your flaws so you can find solutions to them and constantly improve your awareness.

Gratefulness: Before you meditate or engage in other mindful behaviors, start the session with something you are grateful for and think about that for a few moments or write something about it. This helps to condition your mind to feel and appreciate more of the beauty around you.

Continue to challenge yourself throughout your practice by changing the way you sit during meditation, by focusing more on your breath, or by relaxing your body entirely. See if you can keep your focus even in very loud or distracting environments.

Chapter 16: Where To Meditating At Home

If you prefer the solitude of meditating in your own home you certainly aren't alone.There is something Beautiful about finding a quiet and comfortable spot in the safety of a familiar and comfortable place that helps you to begin with a sense of peace. The first thing you will want to do when choosing A spot is be sure that it is free from distractions like television and internet.

Meditating is healthy and can have almost miraculous benefits to your life and your state of mind, but in the beginning it is likely that you will be very prone to distraction. So, be sure not to have the TV on, or to do it in a room that isn't constantly frequented by that obnoxious roommate.The goal is to find (or create) a space that will foster a sense of tranquility. A lot of people prefer to set aside a specific place for meditation that they will return to each time.This is highly recommended! If you have a dedicated spot for meditation and reflection then putting yourself in that frame of mind will slowly become much easier. To this end, it may be good for you to set up an altar, or meditation table, in your new spot.Essentially, this is a small table with the tools of your new trade. You will want to place objects to guide you along your inner journey. These might include a focus, like a candle for a visual focus, or a speaker for listening to some zazen music or for guided meditations, perhaps some images of a current goal, like that pool you have always wanted, or that dream job.Meditation has many different techniques and a meditation table may not be for you, but when you are beginning having a quiet place that you can go to again and again will be a great benefit to you.Aim to have a spot that you consider sacred whether or not you choose to have a meditation table. It really should be a quiet contemplative area where you can relax completely and not be afraid of judgment or interruption.

Meditating outdoors

Understandably, some of us can't meditate at home. It may be because we have children or pets. We might not be able to spend much time at home at all, perhaps traveling for work. If you choose to meditate outdoors then feel free to find or build a nice calming space, perhaps in your garden or under a tree. Personally, I like to hike and there is a spot in my local nature reserve that I make a point to stop and meditate at every time I hike through that area. It can be anywhere as long as it is quiet enough and you are comfortable and it is peaceful enough to look inward.

Meditation Centers

For someone who is more of a hands-on learner, meditation centers may be the perfect arena for honing your new skills. It is a good place to seek out the peace and quiet that you might not be able to put together in your home or find regularly outdoors. They are also great places to connect with people who are walking a similar path as you, or to get in touch with masters who might have the advice you need to hear for someone just starting out, as well as a place to find even more recommended reading.

Here is an excellent resource for finding meditation centers near you that provides for many different styles of meditation with a strong focus on different branches Tibetan Buddhism.

Look for something that fits you personally and feels right.You may even want to try out a few different centers to see what makes sense for your personal efforts. If you live in a less densely populated area this index may not be for you.I would suggest using google to find something near you.Be sure to look over reviews to watch out for scam artists.It is a sad truth but scammers exist in all aspects of society and when people are searching for answers to deep questions involving personal development they are all the more vulnerable. I have personally found 4 great and free meditation centers for myself and others in my area through google searches, it is a valuable tool!

Chapter 17: Quick And Simple Techniques For A Beginner's Practice

Now that you have all the prior knowledge you need, it is time to delve into the practice itself. There are many kinds of meditation techniques that you can get acquainted with, and this chapter will aim to give you as many options as possible to help you start strong.

Fast and Simple: Techniques on the Go

There are just too many people out there who don't have enough time in their hands but still want to practice meditation. Although meditation can be done anywhere and in almost any circumstance, it is important that you start with some beginner-friendly practices that won't take up too much time. All the exercises in this section can be done within 10 minutes, but you can make it last longer if you want.

When you are using certain techniques to fit a certain time frame, you have to put all thought of time constraints out of your head. It would be best if you chose a short time after you wake up or just before you go to bed. Keep in mind that making your mind be still is not easy accomplished, especially for a beginner. But also know that this can become simpler and easier as you go along, so don't let yourself be discouraged by any short-term setbacks.

Basic Meditation with Affirmation

This basic meditation technique is a great way to start your practice. This starts off with the basics and you can add visualizations or added stillness later on.

Step 1.Sit on the floor or on a chair and keep your back as straight as possible withoutstraining yourself. Make sure that you are comfortable and can hold the position for at least 5 minutes. Choose a place where you won't be disturbed.

Step 2.Breathe deeply and relax your body as you breathe. As this is probably your first time, it might be wise to keep your eyes closed throughout the process.

Step 3.Choose a phrase that you would like to affirm in your life. Try to use the first person and make sure it's something meaningful to you. Examples can include "There is peace inside me," "I am worthy of love," or "God watches over me."

Step 4.Take slow measure breaths. Make your breathing as easy and relaxed as possible and empty your mind of other thoughts.

Step 5.Now repeat the affirmation to yourself quietly. Try to focus only on the affirmation. If you do get distracted by random thoughts, allow the thought to pass rather than suppress it. Simply return your attention to the affirmation gently.

Step 6.If you find it difficult to focus with a purely mental effort, you can try to whisper the words to yourself, moving you're tongue without really speaking a word. Join your breathing with your affirmation and repeat the phrase as you breathe out.

Continue this exercise for at least five minutes. Remember not to get frustrated, as your body will end up tensing rather than relaxing. Notice how you felt during the exercise. Was focusing your attention on affirmations and breathing difficult for you? What kinds of thoughts did you find popping into your head?

Focused Breathing

When you can manage to stay focused on affirmations, it is time you focus solely on the breath. This is a great way to develop focused awareness, concentration, and stillness of the mind. Don't expect to have a quiet mind right away. This is all normal and will improve as you continue your practice.

Step 1. Sit comfortably with your back straight in a place where you won't be disturbed.

Step 2. Breathe deeply and relax your body. You can choose to close your eyes or keep them open. However, if you find that your thoughts still have a tendency to race around you, keeping your eyes closed will help keep distractions at the minimal.

Step 3. Turn your attention towards the sensation of your breath. This is a good time to practice the beginner's mind. Experience your breathing as if for the first time. Feel your chest rise and fall as you breathe. Listen intently to the sound of each breath and feel the air enter and leave your body.

Step 4. Continue this meditation for at least 5 minutes. Since you are focusing solely on your breathing, you might find yourself easily distracted by random thoughts and emotions. Don't be alarmed or critical of yourself when this happens. Simply acknowledge the thought or emotion without judgment then let it go. Gently direct your focus back to your breathing.

It would be beneficial for you to continue practicing these techniques before you move on to more complex practices. As the basic core of almost all of the meditation practices involves awareness of the breath and concentration, these techniques are great if you simply want to stay with the basics or if you want to move on and deepen your practice.

Rolling Up your Sleeves: Longer and Deeper Practices

You can liken your mind to a deep lake. If you only look at the surface (the ordinary mind), you're often blind to the wonders underneath. When you start practicing focused awareness, you're actually learning to swim in the waters of your own mind. Once you start getting better at swimming, then you can start diving deeper into the depths.

This section will introduce more intermediate practices that allow you to get a good look into your own psyche. The exercises in this section should be done for 20 minutes or more. You can extend the length of your practice according to your own preference and needs.

Body-Tuning Technique

This technique is one of the most important intermediate techniques in meditation as it gets you back in touch with your body. A great majority of people in society are fragmented. The mind is often torn in fragments of positive and negative emotions that aren't fully explored. Worst of all, the body is disconnected from awareness and the mind. This technique aims to get the mind and body reconnected, and make them whole again.

Step 1. This meditation must be done lying down. Find a flat, solid surface that allows for comfort, but not so much that you can end up drifting off to sleep.

Step 2. Direct your awareness to your body as a whole. Pay attention to every sensation that you feel. Feel the places where your body touches the surface of where you're lying on. Feel the cool breeze that wafts through the room, or the warmth of your own body.

Step 3. After a few minutes of full-body awareness, gently direct your attention towards the biggest toe of your left foot. Feel any and all sensations in this one area. If you don't feel anything, then simply focus on the lack of sensation.

Step 4.Start to visualize your breathe flow in and out of your toe, bringing much needed energy with it. When you're ready, expand your awareness towards your whole left foot and continue to breathe in and out of it. Continue this for at least 2 minutes.

Step 5.When you're done, let your awareness travel upward to your ankles and lower leg. Be patient with yourself and continue visualizing your breath going in and out in waves across this area of your body.

Step 6.From here, go up to your knees and thighs. When you're done with your left leg, go back down and focus on your right fight. Repeat the visualization and focus that you did on your other foot. From here, continue to go higher. From the pelvis, go higher to the abdomen, lower back, the navel, upper back, then the chest and shoulders.

Try to slow down in the areas where there are main organs, such as the lungs, heart, and stomach. Imagine your breath bringing healing energy to your organs. Now bring your focus to your left fingers and hands then up towards your elbows and arms. Repeat the same technique until you've finished with both hands.

From here, bring your awareness to your neck then up to your face. Give special attention to the space right between you're brows. Finally, finish by focusing on the top of your head. The last two areas can be especially receptive. You might end up feeling like your floating and that your consciousness is more fluid in your own body.

Step 7. When you're ready, pull your awareness away from your head and bring your awareness back to your whole body. Feel your breath go in and out in waves.

Step 8. After a few minutes, wriggle your toes and fingers and slowly open your hand. Return your awareness to normal and stretch a little before you get up.

Meditation with Visualizations

Visualizations can be added to your basic meditation techniques and can help develop a certain trait or attitude in you. When practicing certain visualization techniques, simply start off with basic breathing meditation. When you feel at peace and still, you can start your visualization.

The Sanctuary

Visualizing a sanctuary or a refuge is a great place to recharge your energy and shake off some stress and anxiety. This technique can also help in healing certain mental and emotional wounds.

Step 1.Do your standard, basic meditation until your mind is relatively still and your body relaxed (preferably for 5 minutes).

Step 2.Start to visualize a place where you've always felt safe. It might be a real place from your past or just something you imagined. As long as it makes you feel safe and protected then it should work. Be as specific as you want. If you imagine yourself in a garden then what plants can be found there? Are there singing birds and trees that provide shade? Do your best to make the visualization as vivid as possible.

Step 3.Once you've found your safe place, simply allow the sensation of peacefulness, safety and comfort permeate across your entire being. Know that you are safe here, and that no one can touch you here. Within your sanctuary, you can explore all your emotions, even those of hurt, fear and humiliation.

Step 4.Stay in your sanctuary for as long as you need and make sure to end your session by reaffirming the positive emotions you feel in your safe place.

Mindfulness, Anytime, Anywhere

Mindfulness meditation can be done at any time while doing other things. This makes mindfulness one of the best ways to do meditation on the go. As long as you completely pay attention to what you're doing in the present. You have to be able to combine focused awareness with welcoming acceptance. The aim of mindfulness meditation is to have you fully present in whatever you're doing.

Mindful Eating

This is a great mindfulness exercise that you can do at work during your lunch break. Simply find a quiet place and eat your lunch.

Step 1.Appreciate your food as you lay it out in front of you. Think of the effort and hard work that's gone into making your meal.

Step 2.Look and Smell – note the appearance and aroma of your food, be curious and notice everything you can see and smell.

Step 3. Bring the food to your lips and note how it feels against your tongue. Savor the taste of the food as you chew. Take note of all the emotions you feel as you eat.

Step 4. Try to stay mindful throughout the entire meal

Mindfulness can be done along with any other chores and activities as long as you practice focused attention. You can be mindful as you walk down a street or as you clean up around the house. You can even be mindful while talking to a friend or spending time with your family. Mindfulness can only amplify the joy and satisfaction that you feel as you engage in these activities.

Chapter 18: Meditation Can Help You Achieve Your Goal

Essentially, in any case if there are bunches of Meditation Techniques for Beginners, they all have one normal objective and that is to center the brain on a more solid condition of being.

You can accomplish those through different routines yet Meditation for Beginners is truly straightforward. The main affection individuals present why they don't give it a go is on the grounds that they have a troublesome time concentrating. They say that their brains meander off.

This plan can, point of fact, give help with that. It includes joining mindful breathing and origination, things which everybody has the capacity do.

One of the finest methods to "relieve the psyche" is to make your breathing example the point of convergence of your consideration. When you close your eyes and center your regard for your breathing, you can hope to feel your contemplations starting to unwind. Utilizing your nose to breathe in and your mouth to breathe out is the best strategy of doing this.

It's terribly basic to the body that you inhale profoundly. The all the more seriously you inhale, the slower the pace of your pulse. Your body will unwind much more when the measure of oxygen transported to the mind increments and this is a physiological actuality.

It's very discernible that despite the fact that there are diverse Meditation Techniques for Beginners, they all go around a fundamental subject: focusing in on your breath. When you begin having control once again your breathing, then you'll have complete control over your level of anxiety too.

A basic and crucial method incorporated in Meditation for Beginners is perception which happens to be an exceptionally compelling instrument. Science has demonstrated that the mind is crippled to distinguish the distinction between envisioning an activity and truly acting it out. Henceforth in both cases, the cerebrum creates a synthetic that is as what makes the muscles work similarly. Whether the body really does something or not is totally insignificant.

This implies something colossal. Overall, its letting us know that envisioning something has a broad impact on your body. When you get to be capable at consoling your brain through your breathing example, you may incorporate view of the majority of the stuff you wish to have paying little heed to whether its a thing or an inclination.

In case you're examining How to Meditate in light of the fact that you yearning to achieve an easy condition of rest, then you can absolutely imagine things that imply unwinding for you. You can really invoke pictures of the woods, the ocean or anyone of water. You may additionally envision something you can't touch like shafts of hued light, an image or example, or whatever else that puts your psyche very still.

After you get to be capable in Meditation Techniques for Beginners, you may expand your routine by incorporating unwinding music alongside different things identified with reflection. The imperative thing here is to never surrender however rather make contemplation a practice that you basically incorporate inside of your day by day schedule.

Still, never consider contemplation as a commitment. Try not to overlook your body. On the off chance that you don't think you could ruminate, there's dependably a next time. Consider that very much executed reflection that keeps going 10 minutes is constantly better than contemplation finished with an overwhelming heart. Quality as opposed to amount is what's fundamental in reflection.

Chapter 19: Mindfulness Techniques

Ready?

Exercise one: taking an inventory

This is the best exercise to start with. When I asked if you were "ready" above, what was your response? Did you stop, look away from the page, and actually consider whether you felt ready before reading on? Or did your eyes just flick over the word, read it, then move immediately on to the next section?

Well, let's try it again. Are you ready?

Let's "take an inventory" and consider where you are right now, in this very moment. Do a full stock take on your body, heart and mind. How do you feel right now? What thoughts are in your mind? What sensations are in your body? Where is your attention? Notice everything.

You may end up with an assessment that looks like this: "I'm aware of a slight sense of boredom and I feel a little doubtful – I've read so many self help books! When I think this, my jaw tightens. I'm slouching at the moment, and I'm feeling a bit too full after that extra helping of pasta. I feel aggravated still from that conversation earlier on. My mind keeps flicking back to the car alarm blaring outside. I hope this book gets to the good stuff soon…"

As an exercise, do your own inventory now. Yes, right now. There's no better time than the present – in fact, the only time is the present. If you enjoyed this activity (or even if you didn't!) see if you can incorporate it into your life. Do it every morning as a little "check up" to start your day in a mindful way or whip it out when you're feeling flustered and overwhelmed. Do you find it boring? Difficult? Great! Now you have more material to note in your inventory. See how that works? There is no way to mess it up.

Exercise two: getting into the body

When was the last time you used your body?

Think about that for a moment. When last were you fully in your body, stretching it, running, getting your lungs and heart pumping and your sweat pouring? When last were you completely aware of every little part of you, from the top of your head to the tips of your toes?

So many of us work in jobs that only require our mental effort. We entertain ourselves by watching or reading things, and reduce our relationships with others to the verbal communication we exchange. In fact, bodily awareness is often only developed in those who make a career of it – athletes or dancers, for example – as though the rest of us don't even have bodies.

The great thing about the body is that it lives in the present moment, unlike your mind. There is no real way to stress about the future or the past with your arms or legs, right? The way your foot encounters the ground is always right here, right now.

The body is an excellent channel into the present moment. By tuning into the 5 senses of your body, you tune out your overactive mind and invite yourself a little deeper into consciousness of the present moment.

Here is a simple exercise to practice this. It's called "walking" and to be honest, you probably haven't really done it since you were a child. We walk all the time, but with a head full of nonsense, focused on where we're going or where we came from, disconnected to the simple motions happening in the moment.

Go for a walk, for no reason at all. Don't even go for a walk as a mindfulness exercise. Just walk to walk. Don't go anywhere in particular. Go at any speed you like, anywhere you like. Focus on the walking. How does your foot feel as it hits the ground? What is the process of your body shifting your weight across the surface of that foot, and how does it flow rhythmically? What does it feel like to have a spine? What are your arms doing?

What does the air do as it enters your nostrils and swirls around in your lungs?

If you like, become conscious of squirrels in the bushes or the sound of tarmac crunching a little under the rubber of your shoe. Resist the urge to rate your walk as good or bad, just calmly ask all your senses to focus on the walking.

Your noisy mind will want to butt in. Possibly every half second or so! Don't stress, this is what it's done all its life. When it does, look at the thought, think, "OK" and then bring your attention back to the walking. It doesn't matter if 10 minutes go by before you realize you got distracted with thinking about Christmas shopping or work gossip. When you realize your thoughts have trailed off, just be aware and come back to your walking and to your body.

Exercise three: pause

I think that for some people, their lives are like badly written essays without any punctuation. No full stops, no commas, no spaces between paragraphs. Just a wall of endless text.

Being mindful is like putting punctuation into your crazy thought traffic and making things flow a little better. Like putting those vital empty spaces back into the story of your life. For this exercise, you're going to get into the habit of putting full stops in things. It's the equivalent of hitting the enter key a few times, resetting things and taking a moment to step back and just look at life for a second.

Right now, just unplug and take a step back. At the end of this paragraph, forget about the book for a bit and focus your entire being on the simple task of taking a few cleansing breaths, nothing more. Whenever you feel tired, angry, stressed, anxious or unhappy, this will give you some literal breathing room and some space to welcome the present moment back into your awareness.

You can say, "wow, I'm really getting carried away here." How many people do you know who wind themselves up more and more, each thought feeding on the previous one, getting into a froth of emotion that later makes them say things like, "I don't know what came over me."

Well, this pausing exercise is like an emotional fuse. It snaps you out of the flurry of thought and emotion loops and is the beginning of truly deep mindfulness. It's one thing to be aware and focused when you have a free hour and some cushions and incense – but can you do it in the middle of a stressful traffic jam when you're late? Can you do it when you've just had a sad conversation with a friend? When you're bored and open the fridge for some edible entertainment?

Speaking of cushions and incense, these brief moments of mindfulness will also act as a bridge to more formal mediation, which we'll consider later in this guide. For now, build in as many little mindfulness windows into your day as you can remember to, or whenever you feel yourself getting "carried away."

Exercise four: change the channel

Like Leah, you may be stuck in a rut. The universe is vast and unfolding magnificently all around you, and yet you only ever tread the same tired old routes you always have. This could be eating the same things over and over, thinking the same things over and over, and having a boring routine. This means dating the same kind of person over and over again, sitting in the same spot in the living room, wearing the same clothes you always do, taking the same path to work every day... you get the picture.

Stress tends to drive us in ever-decreasing circles. It's easy to end up like a hamster trapped in its wheel, forever running but never getting anywhere. You can step outside such stressful cycles by consciously breaking some of your most ingrained habits.

This is a bit like the pausing exercise above, only you are taking some breathing room from life in general. Break your routines and you'd be surprised at what fresh perspectives come flooding in. In our story, Leah felt unimpressed with life. Instead of curiosity and wonder, she was mostly bored or irritated with things, and felt that nothing was really enjoyable anymore.

Switching perspectives, though, opens up new and unused avenues of awareness, ones that are literally right under your nose. Creativity, joy and spontaneity all occur when we let go of stale old ideas of life and have the courage to let things just be. Today, try a very simple perspective-switching exercise. Sit in a different chair. You can stop there, noting if you feel different for doing so, or you could take it further.

Lay on your living room floor and look at it from the perspective of an ant. Have you really looked at your apartment lately? Sleep on the other side of the bed. Sleep naked if you usually don't or with fancy pajamas if you usually sleep naked. Take a different route to work or wear a color you never wear. Go watch a movie but only choose which one when you arrive, spontaneously.

Take it even further, if you like. Try on different opinions and ideas for size. Argue on the other side of the debate to the one you're used to. Read something you might disagree with. Do the opposite of what you usually do, just to see what will happen. See what it feels like to say, "thank you" when complimented instead of arguing back. Read a book you never thought you would. Go out walking and keep going until you encounter a place you never have before.

You can take this exercise as far as you like. It doesn't matter how far, though – what matters is that you're deliberately changing things up, and deliberately welcoming in a fresh perspective. This kick starts a new appreciation of something full and beautiful that's always been there: the present moment.

Exercise five: forego the unreal for the real

There is nothing beside the present moment. Try to really feel that right now. Truly, all your stress about things that happened years ago? None of that exists anymore. Literally, the only thing that remains of it are your thoughts. Similarly, the future is unreal — it's nothing but thoughts. And thoughts can change!

The only thing that is concrete and real right now for any of us is the present moment. Are you in your living room right now, reading this? Your chair, your hands and feet, the blood in your veins, the smile on your lips, your partner sitting across from you — these things are real. For all intents and purposes, nothing else exists except these things.

And if you don't notice them? Then they don't exist at all.

When you forego all this exuberant reality and choose instead to get lost in unreal thoughts about the past or the future, you pluck yourself right out of reality. That beautiful, ever-refreshing moment is wasted. You lose out.

How could you ever do any self development if you're not even used to being yourself? How could you work on relationships with other people you scarcely notice? How can you get what you want in life when you have never taken the time to perceive what that actually is?

This exercise is about switching your focus from unreal to real perceptions. Of course, we all need to make plans for the future, and to look at the past and make adjustments according to what we've learnt. But on the balance, most of us spend relatively little time on the real moment right in front of us.

Find some time today to forgo unreal ruminations for real things in the moment. Instead of getting distracted thinking about how many calories you've eaten that day, become aware of the plate of food sitting right in front of you. Are you hungry? What sensations are in your body as you eat?

Instead of waiting for someone to stop talking so you can jump in and say your bit, really focus on what's real: the words coming out of their mouths right at that moment. Really listen. Instead of buying a book about Buddhism from Amazon, stop and take a breath. Do something real. Smell the air. Look at a simple flower like Buddha did and see what you see there.

This may be a strange and difficult exercise to do at first, but once you make the subtle distinction, you may find you actually enjoy re-orienting to the real and the present. There is something very calming and grounding about tuning into what is, rather than what could or should be.

Exercise six: gratitude

So far, our exercises have primarily focused on building awareness. Awareness is its own reward and has a funny way of growing bigger and bigger the more you practice it. But for this exercise, lets take our growing sense of awareness and do something deliberately positive with it.

Like Leah, the joy and sparkle may seem to have drained from your life. This is because as the present moment is hurtling by unnoticed, it takes with it all those potential moments of bliss and beauty and wonder. By becoming more mindful, you also give yourself the opportunity to discover all these little gifts you may have missed before.

For this exercise, you may wish to jot thoughts down in a journal or just meditate on your responses. Practice being grateful today. Don't make up things to be happy about, just become aware of little pockets of happiness you've never noticed before.

Which activities, things or people in your life make you feel good? Can you give additional appreciative attention and time to these activities? Gently resolve to pay them more attention today.

Can you pause for a moment when pleasant moments occur? Help yourself pause by noticing your body sensations, your thoughts and feelings. Savor those moments.

Can you immerse fully in pleasant moments and then release them when they are over?

Exercise seven: the power of ritual

Ordinarily, ritual and routine are the places where mindfulness goes to die. We've already seen that staying in boring ruts kills that precious sense of alertness to the moment. But there are ways to use ritual and routine to your advantage.

By making mindfulness a habit just like our other habits, we build in moments where we almost automatically switch to a mindful state. For example, everybody eats every day, and so building a mindfulness ritual around eating ensures that you're never more than a few hours away from finding that calm state again.

Food preparation is also a great opportunity for mindfulness – enlist your vision, hearing, taste, smell and touch to really get deep into the moment. Focus on the feel of the knife as it slices through vegetables of different texture, or the smell released as each vegetable is chopped. You may find this brings indescribably joy to even mundane things, and has the side effect of making you slow down and do things well.

Become a model citizen! When crossing the street, use the pedestrian signals as an opportunity to stand quietly and focus on your breath, rather than an opportunity to try to beat the lights.

You can make mindfulness rituals out of anything: bathing and grooming are excellent for this, as is your daily commute, getting dressed, cleaning your kitchen, stretching before bed or after you wake up. You may even try something creative like putting a colored band on your arm. When you see it, take a breath and become mindful. Eventually, you may slip into this mindful state automatically, and without effort.

Today, look at your life and all the things you do routinely every day. Look for places to insert moments of alert mindfulness and practice working this state of mind into your real, everyday life.

Chapter 20: Practising Mindfulness Meditation

This book includes an exercise which is very beneficial to your concentration levels. The reason for this is to explain how powerful meditation can be. If you find yourself in a middle of a busy day with not enough energy to get through the afternoon, then try this exercise because it will strengthen the way that you feel.

If you can find a space which is calm and relaxing, this helps. It could be a park or a garden. It could simply be an empty conference room away from the noise and bustle of life. You need to have something with you that you can focus on or you can use an element which is already in that room.

Sit comfortably because this is vital. If your body hurts in the position you choose to sit in, then your powers of concentration will automatically be diverted to your pain. Your clothing should be loose and cause no discomfort. Focus your eyes on an object and make sure that they do not wander to look at other things. This is why it's vital to choose somewhere where there is little distraction. Your eyes are slightly lowered as you observe the object.

Now, breathe in through the nostrils, one at a time if you like to the count of eight. Hold the breath inside of you for the count of 10. As you breathe out from the diaphragm, count to 15. If you can't manage 15 try a lesser number and increase it as and when you are ready.

These breathing exercises help the levels of oxygen in the body. They help you to reach a level where you are fully alert and able to carry on with your day with a renewed strength. Practising this exercise is the first step into the world of mindful meditation and will help you to reap benefits fairly quickly.

The things that you need to look out for are:

- Distractions

- Discomfort
- Not breathing correctly
- Counting the breath time

If you are distracted, the system is unlikely to work. However, there is nothing to stop you trying again if time permits. Discomfort will catch you out, so don't skip that part of the exercise. Make sure you are comfortable to gain maximum benefit from the exercises. If you find that you are not breathing correctly or lose count, start again. People who are new to this kind of breathing may find it a little strange at first, but practice will improve their methods.

Counting the breath times is vital to making this work. Get more oxygen circulating in your body and feel the energy. Be aware of your breathing and savor every moment of it while concentrating the eyes on your chosen object.

This cuts off the possibility of your eyes being distracted and filling your mind with information which gets in the way of relaxation.

Chapter 21: What Is Mindfulness?

Life is full of distractions, and the mind is often disturbed and it may feel lost from time to time. Practising mindfulness is to bring back the power of focus, finding peace among chaos and have self-confidence in facing difficulties in day-to-day living; being still within when there are noises without. Nevertheless, outcomes of practising mindfulness for each individual may not be the same even though practices of mindfulness are all based on same principles. Whatever circumstance may be, the objective of mindfulness is to seek rest and courage from our fears and challenges by look for resources inwardly. The purpose of this book is to offer some useful mindfulness practices, which are relevant for today's working professionals, to enhance self-confidence and self-esteem through recommended activities; to empower individuals to be self-driven, self-motivated and ready to overcome and achieve greater things in their lives.

Therefore, let's take a closer look at the fundamental question: what is mindfulness?

Mindfulness is the act of paying attention to your thoughts and feelings with no intention of changing and judging it.

Your awareness of what are going on inside your mind and your external world are important. While some people choose not to be bothered about their inner feelings, mindfulness seek to create a balance by relating both internal and external elements. Paying attention to things like tastes, smells, emotions, sensations, sounds and whatever that are going on in your surroundings and inside you at the present moment enables you to reason rationally and act appropriately in a calm manner. Just be mindful of your inner feelings and thoughts without judgement, for it is the easiest and most rewarding exercise which you can take part in.

MECHANISMS OF MINDFULNESS

Mindfulness is not a new practice, for even before the dawn of civilization, it has been commonly practised by ancient masters of meditation for hundreds of years. The aim of mindfulness is to observe one's thoughts as an outsider and bring all emotions and feelings of the human mind and heart to a state of peace, rest and quietness. Mindfulness is usually initiated by an intention of no judgement, characterized by an attention of careful observation and implemented by an attitude of compassion. The implication of compassionate mindfulness is when you are observing your own feelings, emotions, thoughts and present environments without commenting right or not to yourself and allowing them to happen. You may choose to quiet your feelings and emotions but to choose to observe them will bring enlightenment to your soul. Knowing that it is not possible for you to shut off yourself instantly from noises of the external world, so just being aware and be mindful of what is happening around you will eventually enlighten you to an answer which you are searching for regardless of where you are, whether you are in a meeting or doing your daily work at your desk or having a coffee-break, for the answer will come when you are at rest within. Mindfulness allows you to identify and accept any feelings you have inside yourself; it allows you to be more aware of your environment and also allows you to decide on how your reaction and your attitude should be towards your current situation in a positive and constructive way. The concept of mindfulness can be regarded as a kind of introspection, whereby an individual may confront with challenges that may affect his rational thinking processes and the practice of mindfulness creates the essential space of meditation until there is stillness within, and the excellent outward performance is an outcome of a normal reflection of the inward peace of the mind. People may prefer to ignore any reflection on their present thoughts, yet that there is great gain in reflective thinking. There are many digital distractions today, but if you are willing, you are often able to obtain relieve from your innermost disturbance when you take time to engage in mindfulness exercise.

Chapter 22: Breathing Techniques

The importance of breathing correctly is often overlooked as it is an automatic process and yet breathing energises, fuels and detoxifies. Most people do not breathe as deeply as they should and shallow breathing is not sufficient. When your students fail to breathe fully, they miss out on improved heart and lung function, greater immune system health and clarity of mind.

Task 1:
Ask your students what they believe to be the benefits of breathing correctly.

This opens up an interesting debate and interactive session. Discuss all of the suggestions given and tick them off the list and then relay the final benefits by discussing those listed below. If you engage the students, they will remain fixed in the present throughout and will be in a mindful state.

Task 2:

Once you have discussed all of the benefits ask students, either in pairs or individually, to write down a list of benefits. Some will struggle to retain the information and others will become distracted. Afterwards, remind them of the benefits of mindfulness in terms of memory retention and learning.

Go through each of the benefits:

1. 70% of the body's toxins are released through breathing. For those who do not breathe correctly, they are not removing the toxins within which could lead to illness. Carbon dioxide is exhaled and this

is the natural waste of your body's metabolism.

2. Breathing aids the release of tension. Shallow breathing does not provide sufficient levels of oxygen.
3. Brain oxygenation reduces anxiety levels, it also brings clarity.
4. When uneasy feelings are experienced, breathing correctly can help to alleviate emotional problems.

5. Breathing is a natural pain reliever. When you breathe into your pain, it helps to ease it.
6. Diaphragm movements during deep breathing massages the stomach, small intestine, liver and pancreas. Vital organs are massaged, this increases circulation and controlled breathing also serves to strengthen and tone up those abdominal muscles.

7. Breathing sends oxygen to all of the body's cells, and this strengthens the muscles of the body.
8. Oxygen enrichens your body and metabolises all those important nutrients

and vitamins.

9. Breathing improves posture. When bad posture is present, this affects the quality of breathing.

10. Deep breathing increases oxygen in the blood, improves the quality of blood and removes carbon dioxide.

11. Breathing has a direct, positive effect on digestion and food assimilation. The organs of the digestive system receive more oxygen.

12. Breathing nourishes the brain, spinal cord and nerves and this increases health and well-being to the whole body.

13. When you breathe deeply, your lungs are strengthened, this also reduces the risk of respiratory health problems.

14. By breathing correctly, the heart becomes stronger and the lungs work more efficiently.

15. Breathing techniques help to increase energy levels and stamina.

16. Breathing helps to elevate mood.

17. When breathing correctly, the extra oxygen helps to burn up excess fat or for

those who are underweight, the oxygen fuels tissues and glands.
Task:
Talk your students through the correct breathing process as below:

To be able to breathe properly, it's important to breathe into the abdomen and not just the chest area. Inhalation and exhalation should be slow, deep and rhythmic. Breathe in through the nose and not the mouth.

☐ Sit comfortably and then inhale through the nose, expanding the belly and then filling the chest.
☐ Count to 5 for this process.
☐ Hold the breath for a count of 3.
☐ Exhale through the mouth for a count of 5.
☐ Perform at least two rounds of this breathing technique each day.

Note: To ensure correct breathing students can place their hands on their abdomens and they will feel the movement as their stomachs extend. By staying focused on their breathing students naturally become mindful. In addition, they will start to feel more peaceful.

Task:

This is a fun breathing technique for students but it has many health benefits including: vitality, clarity of mind, it tones the digestive system and, improves digestion. It also improves the liver, pancreas, spleen and abdominals.

Bellows breath

This technique involves the individual breathing in and out rapidly (through the nose) and when done correctly, it improves feelings of vitality. Aim for three breaths in and out per second.

Note: This should be practiced for 15 seconds only in the first instance so to prevent hyperventilation. The duration can be extended (slowly) as the body adjusts. Maximum duration is 60 seconds from start to finish.

This should be not done by those with epilepsy, seizures or panic disorders. If there is any possibility of pregnancy, this breathing technique should be avoided.

Breathing for stress

Re-centring breathing is ideal for moments of stress.

Students often feel the pressure of stress and expectancy during exam times and re-centring is the perfect mindfulness techniques to help them relax. It's not difficult to do, but practice is essential and it is important to utilise this breath during times of difficulty. It simply aids control.

Task:

Students should sit in a comfortable position (in the chair) and have their feet flat on the floor.

They should rest their hands on the top of their thighs and then close their eyes. Breathe normally through the nose but this time, focus on the air that is coming in and out of the body. As they visualise the air (especially) on the out breath, they should then breathe slowly.

After this mindful breathing process, they must ask themselves how they feel. What they noticed during this time and if they feel any calmer.
Note: There are no right or wrong answers

Students should repeat the breathing technique, inhaling slowly and steadily through the nose, then exhaling slowly through the mouth.

During the inhalation, they must think 'breathing in' and on the exhalation, they must think, 'breathing out'. All other thoughts should be accepted but then pushed aside. Continue this breathing pattern for 10 rounds and then they should question how they feel.

This re-centering technique enables the individual to calm down and to enable them to think with greater clarity.
Task:

Belly breathing is a useful technique for all age as follows:

Breathe in slowly for 4 seconds (through the nose)

Students must pretend they are blowing up an imaginary balloon which is placed in their stomach and to imagine the balloon inflating as they do so. They should then pause for two seconds holding the breath and then exhale through the mouth.

Students must try to visualise the balloon deflating. Wait for two seconds and then repeat. It's important to keep shoulders and chest relaxed and still throughout. The work is done in the abdomen.

Mindful Meditation

It takes very little time each day to meditate and it is certainly an important element to mindfulness. Some might say it's the core component to a mindfulness practice and although not difficult, it takes time and practice to make meditating fairly easy. It can take as little as 10 minutes to still the mind and to ensure the mind is focused on the present only. Remember that to be mindful requires an awareness of thoughts and actions in a non-judgemental manner in the present.

There has been much research undertaken into the benefits of a mindful meditation and certainly mindfulness students state there is often enhanced mood, less stress and a general feeling of wellbeing.

Note that some students may find it difficult to sit still and to allay any errant thoughts for a period of 10 minutes so initially, if necessary, try for five minutes and then increase. It can be a good idea to provide a guided meditation in the first instance as this will then enable you to talk the students though the process. Alternatively, there are guided meditations available and these can be a powerful resource to ignite interest and to keep the students attention in place. With practice, mindful meditation becomes easier and can be expanded.

Task:

Students should find a comfortable seated position and ensure that their backs are straight (but not tense) and that the head and neck is in alignment. They should not be in a slumped position.

Although thoughts of the past, present and future may bombard their minds, they should push all thoughts to one side. They should think only of the present moment and become aware of their breathing, focusing only on the sensation of the air as it moves in and out of their body.

The focus should move to the abdomen as it expands on the inhalation and then how the abdomen reduces as the air is expelled.

The attention then is on the breath and how each one is a little different. Turning the attention inwards enables them to check how their body feels throughout.

Students should become aware of the breath, now focusing on the air as it moves in and then out of the body. Feel the abdomen extend and fall. This quiet stillness of five or 10 minutes of focusing on the breath and of remaining in the present forms the basics of mindfulness meditation.

Note: some people have stated that they feel emotional, that they experience a raw energy or that thoughts are bombarding them constantly. This is natural.

In time, they can add to the meditation, extending their abilities, taming difficult or problematic emotions and increasing feelings that are far more beneficial. They can problem-solve, identify issues, view situations with a detached curiosity or they can self-heal, imagining the breath a beautiful healing blue colour. Or they can focus on one sound while meditating, perhaps that of bird song through the window. Nothing else exists barr the individual and the melodic song.

Fear

It's impossible to go through life without experiencing fear of some sort. S tudents may worry about failure, fear of unacceptance or even fear of inadequacy. Fear is a primal emotion and, is essential for survival. It can be a very disconcerting feeling. By practising meditation regularly (daily) it can help the individual to maintain balance even whilst in the midst of fear. It enables them to take a moment to discern whether fear is real or simply a threat and it enables them to view situations with greater clarity. It's then possible to name the fear and this is often detracts from its power.

Recognising that fear is present is very important if the student is going to be able to control it. Common signs are when the chest tightens, heart rate increases or breathing becomes more rapid. At this point, they should take some slow and deep breaths to help slow the body down and acknowledge the fear.

If the students connect deeply with the breathing technique, they will then be able to create space between the emotion and themselves and to identify and understand where the fear has come from and recognise it as such. By naming it they reduce its power avoiding the intensity of any emotional reaction.

In mindfulness it is important that the feeling is acknowledged and worked with. When we feel afraid, for whatever reason, we often become judgemental towards our own, sometimes irrational responses. With mindfulness, we are non-judgemental and so will approach any emotion with friendliness or even a gentle curiosity.

Importantly this approach teaches students to be kind to themselves - whatever their emotion. Once they have faced fear in their mind, they will feel greater confidence and develop an ability to be able to cope with future fears if and when they surface.

Chapter 23: How To Practice Mindful Meditation

Before we look at how to practice mindful meditation, you first need to understand the basics. The two most important things you must bring to mind when engaging in mindful meditation are the time of practice and place. Choosing an appropriate time and place will ensure you practice without external influences and distractions.

Other factors you should consider include the duration, reasons for embarking on this mindful technique, and the necessary steps you should follow when you are new to this practice.

Below are the steps you should take to get the best from your 5 minutes practice as a beginner:

Come up with a strong motivating reason why you would want to make mindful meditation a daily habit.Beating stress should be appropriate here. The reason will act as the motivating force to get you started and keep you going when the practice becomes tiresome.

Think about one major cause of stress in your life. There has to be one problem that initiates the stress response in you more than any other thing. Think about all the problems that could be responsible for your increased stress levels and pick one of them. You do not have to settle on the biggest of them all; in fact, thinking of the biggest may cause a discouragement. At the same time, avoid picking the most insignificant problem since that problem might not be serious enough to motivate you to attain full mindfulness as a way of eliminating the problem to beat stress. Aim to strike a balance.

Bring the problem you have chosen to mind in vivid details. Imagine every scenario that could associate with the problem you have chosen. For instance, if you have chosen your relationship problems, think of all the physical, verbal, psychological, and sexual abuses you suffer in the relationship. If you have chosen your financial problem, think about all the bills you cannot pay because of your financial woes, think about the opportunities you have missed because of lack of funds, think about how depressed and stressed the situation leaves you whenever you think about it.

Become mindful of your feelings and sensations. Can you feel the stress in your body as you think about these things? Take note of feelings such as physical tension, increased heart rate, increased sweating, and notice if you have any butterflies in your stomach. Can you feel any tightness in your jaw, shoulders, or back? Look out for the slightest stress sign/signal and take note of it.

Tune in fully to your emotions. Take note of how you feel. Take note of every emotion you feel and where you feel them in your body. Make sure you try to spot these emotions as much as you can. The more accurate you are at locating these stress signals and emotions in your body, the more mindful you become of your stress levels, and their signals. Spend at least 5 minutes doing this and as you accustom to the practice, increase the duration.

Involve other mindful attitudes. You have to incorporate mindful attitudes such as acceptance, curiosity, and friendliness to your emotions as you practice for increased results. Do not judge or question any feeling. Simply take them all in and accept them.

Touch where you feel any sensation.Touching the part of your body where you feel anything is a friendly gesture that represents kindness to yourself. If you do not succeed at first, do not get discouraged. Just do this in the same way you would place your hands on an injured child with all the care, love, and affection you can muster.With time and practice, you will get better at this.

Be mindful of your breath. Your mindful meditation practice will not be complete without being mindful of your breath.

Align your breath with the sensations from your body. This alignment fosters a mindful attitude and present-moment awareness.

End the session mindfully. You can time yourself with a stopwatch or clock. Once the 5-minuts lapse, end the meditation. With more practice, the 5 minutes will no longer suffice for this exercise, and you will have to increase the duration until you can meditate for 30 minutes or more.

Chapter 24: Simple Exercise To Start With

Watching Your Breath:

This is a simple version of a classic meditation exercise and it's a very good one to begin with.

Before you start your breathing exercise, do a couple of slow deep breaths while holding one hand gently on your diaphragm below your ribs. Did you feel your belly rise? Most people won't feel any real pressure under their hand because most people take only shallow breaths most of the time. This stops our system getting as much oxygen as it could and reduces the benefits we get from each breath. If you start to breath more deeply during the meditation sessions, you

will carry that good habit over to the rest of your day. Don't force your breath down or out. Just try to breathe gently and take in a little more than you used to. Breathing through your mouth is fine but you will find that it becomes dry if you do that for a whole session of twenty minutes or more.

It's better and also usually more comfortable to breathe in through your nose and out through your mouth if you don't have a condition which makes that difficult.

You will benefit from this exercise in several ways. If you have not been doing any type of regular exercise, it will help you to become used to making that part of your day. You will also find that these sessions will let you focus better on how our body is working.

The small step of taking deeper breaths

can help you get more oxygen into your system.

Remember that your rate of progress will vary over time. Learning a new process is rarely a smooth journey.

Because you are just starting to do meditation, make it easier for yourself by finding somewhere that is comfortable, quiet and where you will not be interrupted.

As you progress, you will be able to deal with more distracting external elements. But, avoiding them during the first few weeks gives you a better experience.

When you are ready to start your meditation, decide where you will sit.

A straight chair or the floor are good choices. Put a mat underneath your legs if the floor is cold. Make sure there are no drafts or other factors which could affect your comfort and concentration.

Over time, you will develop your ability to focus on your meditation and not be affected by those factors so much.

Keep your back straight but not rigid. Relax without slouching. You can close your eyes if it helps you to focus on your breath and get less distracted by outside factors.

Some people lay down for their meditation sessions but I found I would fall asleep! That was time wasted because I did not sleep long enough to benefit from it and I needed to take time from something else so that I did the same number of sessions that week.

Please do not rush any stage of your meditation routine.

The important thing is to go through each stage and really connect with your body and the breath which passes through it. Let yourself relax and enjoy the experience. That will help you to have better results and be more comfortable with your meditation.

The biggest distraction is often the constant rush of thoughts racing through our mind. The meditation sessions will help us to eliminate some of them and learn to exercise more control over the rest.

When you are comfortable, focus on the area below your nose and take a gentle deep breath. Don't force anything. Now, follow the air as it moves down through your throat and deep into your lungs.
Wait for a few seconds and focus on how you feel.
Then, let the air slowly move back up and out through your mouth.

If you have a condition which means it is more comfortable to breath through your mouth and not your nose, that won't stop you from benefitting from the exercise.

Do about ten breaths with a few seconds pause between them.
It's important to focus on the process and not be worried about whether you are doing it exactly right or starting to get any benefit from it.
That could lead you back to accepting

negative thoughts which are always around you.

Chapter 25: Mindfulness Meditation Step-By-Step

When you begin this type of meditation, you do need to be away from people and distractions. This helps you to get the hang of meditating but when you are more experienced, you can use mindfulness meditation in other areas of your life even when you are in the company of others. For the simplicity of the exercise, we need to create a certain ambiance. Thus being alone in a quiet place will help you to start this journey. You need to be dressed in comfortable clothing and to be seated in a position that respects your posture.

Step One – Seating position

The pose that you take depends upon your mobility. If you are able to sit on a cushion on a yoga mat, then you would be expected to bend your knees and cross your ankles. Your back should be straight at all times.

If you are unable to sit on the floor because of lack of mobility, that doesn't matter. Find a hard chair and sit with your feet flat on the floor and place your hands in your lap. If you have a chair that leans backward, try to sit with your back straight up because posture is very important.

You do not have to close your eyes although if you wish to, you can light a candle to give you something to focus on.

Step Two – Concentrate on your breathing and position

Be aware of your leg position and your arm position. Be aware of your seating position and don't stiffen your back. Yes, you need to have it straight, but not stiff. Be aware of how your body feels. Start to breathe in through the nostrils and feel the energy going down into your body. Your upper abdomen forms a kind of pivot motion when you get the breathing at the right kind of rhythm. Breathe in and out and get the rhythm to your breathing even and controlled. Feel your body relax. Feel your mind relax.

Step three – Listen to the silence

Silence may be broken from time to time by interference from outdoor noises, the song of a bird or anything that happens within the moment that you are meditating. Accept the silence and also acknowledge and accept the interruptions, letting them simply be acknowledged and then let go of.

Step Four – Relax your eyes

Lower your eyes a little so you don't have to stare. Let them simply be aware of the world around you without having to search anything out. Let them relax.

Step Five – Be kind to your wandering mind

Expect your mind to wander. There is no need to analyze what you are thinking. Simply accept the thought that enters your head and then acknowledge it. Don't let it enter your mind to such a degree that it is able to touch your emotions. Observe it and then let it go without using any kind of judgment at all. No matter what the thought is or what made it arise, simply acknowledge and let go.

Step 6 – Using your breathing to help you concentrate

The central focus during mindfulness meditation is your breath. If you find that this distracts you rather than helping you concentrate on the flame of the candle and when thoughts come into your mind, go back to that candle flicker and rest your mind. It is better if you can get back to the breathing being your focus because this is something you always have with you all the time and you can use this for meditating when you are in other places and want to allow your mind the benefit of meditation.

When you are distracted, go through the process of:

Acknowledgment

Looking without judging

Letting go

Getting back to your focus on your breathing.

When should you meditate?

You can make this something to start your day and meditate before breakfast. Simply set your alarm a little earlier and meditate before the world has woken up and come to life. You should never meditate after eating as you may have to deal with digestive problems. Another time that is good for mindful meditation is at sunset or before your evening meal.

How long to meditate

It's a good idea to make meditation part of your daily routine. Don't expect to find miraculous results straight away. You need time to get your mind accustomed to this way of behaving but the more you do it on a regular basis, the better you will become at it. I would suggest 20 minutes is quite sufficient for beginners and that more experienced meditators can choose their own amount of time.

At the end of meditation

Remember that your body and mind have slowed down. Your blood pressure will be lower and your heartbeat slower. Thus, when you finish meditation for the day, be slow to get back to your normal speed of living. I would use this time to write in a journal the things you can do in your next meditation practice to make your meditation better. This gives you time to transition back into your everyday life.

Conclusion

Thank you again for downloading this book!I hope this book was able to help you to get the idea that almost anything you do can be a mindfulness exercise.The next step is for you to exercise on how to focus on mindfulness.Always remember that you can bring about mindfulness to anything you do, and in so doing, will find yourself less anxious and more prepared in the process.

With honesty, I, just like the 99% of the human race, am very prone to mindlessness. It is extremely common for our minds to drift, to lose focus of what is going on and subsequently lose sight of what is important. But, I firmly believe that mindfulness can be a savior in times of trouble.Sure, it isn't the easiest thing to achieve, but mindfulness will come with time and patience.

In my case, it has helped me prevent an anxiety attack.Had I not utilized mindfulness at that time, I would have probably ended up with a sick daughter having no one to attend to her needs at the hospital, and I would have been so unproductive and still not met my deadlines. Likewise, it may help you a great deal in overcoming your unproductiveness and churning out better results in all walks of life.

Mindfulness cannot solve all our problems.But it has the power to lessen our troubles.Its ultimate goal is to assist us in finding happiness in this world.This book merely touches the tip of the iceberg as far as mindfulness is concerned.There is definitely much more in store for us as we carry on the journey in learning this skill.

I pray you use the simple instructions I shared with you in this book.In so doing, feel free to explore other options to hone your skill.You may also use this with other holistic methods of relaxation.But as you learn to live for the moment, you will eventually see the beauty that each day brings.

Life brings you not just challenges. Life also brings you little joys that are so simple that we often do not recognize them. You will learn to wake up each day with a smile and the excitement of facing a new day of life. It no longer matters if there be some thorns with the roses that life throws at you.

You will learn to have a grateful heart. As you awaken your senses, you will see things that had always been around you but had been hidden in plain view. You will savor the sweet together with the sour taste of food. You will feel the delicate softness of things as well as its roughness.

Treasuring each moment with the help of mindfulness will guide you to find contentment that is quite rare in the world today. With contentment and a grateful heart, you will find yourself threading towards the eternal goal of every human being, and that is, to have happiness in life.